8/22/95

# Surprising Gift

## The Story of Holden Village, Church Renewal Center

D1007312

56 - *Richard L rode*
65 - *John Schramm*
90
73
129 - *Holden is community*

# Charles P. Lutz

*Lutheran Church in America*

**Holden Village Press • Chelan, Washington**

**SURPRISING GIFT**
**The Story of Holden Village, Church Renewal Center**

Library of Congress Catalog Card No. 87-81493
International Standard Book No. 0-9618617-0-3

Manufactured in the U.S.A.

# Contents

## Cover

The cover painting is a watercolor of Holden's mainstreet by Rudolph Wendelin. A Village guest in 1981 and 1983, Rudy recently retired from a career as a graphics specialist with the U.S. Forest Service, Washington, D.C. He was custodian and adapter of the Smokey the Bear image for the Forest Service.

Other books authored or edited by Charles P. Lutz:

*A Christian's Dictionary* (with James S. Kerr, 1969)
*You Mean I Have a Choice?* (1971)
*The Draft and the Rest of Your Life* (with Richard Killmer, 1972)
*Farming the Lord's Land* (1980)
*Peaceways* (with Jerry Folk, 1983)
*Church Roots* (1985)
*Abounding in Hope* (1985)
*God, Goods, and the Common Good* (1987)

*Dedicated . . .*

*to all Holden Village volunteers,
without whose gift of loving labor
the gift of Holden could not continue*

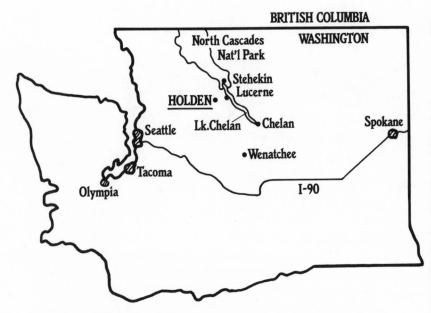

**HOLDEN VILLAGE** is located in north central Washington state.

# Introduction

*If we ever understood this place, we'd spoil it!*
*—Hortie Christman*

Proposals that the story of Holden Village as a church renewal center be told in book form have been made periodically
over the past 20 years. Dr. Merton Strommen, a board member,
suggested at its 1967 meeting that the board commission a
history of the Village. A few years later the board talked about
having a book prepared as part of the 10th anniversary ob-
servance it was planning for 1971. A formal proposal from an
outside writer came to the board at its 1978 meeting but no
action was taken. Board discussion at the time suggested that
no Holden book should be attempted with board approval except by a writer who had known the Village over a long period
of time.

Indeed, in the Village leadership there have always been
some voices speaking words of skepticism about the very idea
of putting on paper the meaning of the phenomenon that is
Holden. Often quoted in such discussions was a word attributed
to Hortie Christman, a Village regular in the 1960s: "If we
ever understood this place, we'd spoil it!"

This effort to produce a book about the Village is undertaken with full respect for the danger of trying to explain Holden. At the same time, the present writer agrees fully with the Holden board that there is a responsibility to preserve in popular form the story of how Holden came to be, both for those who as veteran guests or staff know the Village well and for those who have never been able to visit but wonder why it so captivates its thousands of friends.

## Which Birthday?

The book originated with me on the Fourth of July 1986 when two of the Holden board officers, President Duane Lansverk and Secretary Charlie Mays, asked me to undertake the project. The board had agreed at its just-ended meeting to seek a writer for a book to be ready by the summer season of 1987. One reason for the 1987 target was that some Holdenites considered the summer of 1962 to be the beginning of the Village as a functioning church center for renewal; therefore Holden would celebrate the conclusion of its first quarter century of service the summer of 1987.

But there is at least mild dispute about the year which deserves to be counted the birthday of Holden as a church entity. Three primary candidates seem to be on the ballot:

- 1960, when the gift of the Village was made by Howe Sound Mining Company and received by Seattle's Lutheran Bible Institute;
- 1961, when Holden Village was incorporated and the Forest Service issued a special-use permit, a young-adult summer work program began renovations, and four weeks of LBI-sponsored programing were provided;
- 1962, when the first summer program planned by the national Lutheran youth boards was offered.

An argument could also be made that the birth of Holden as an intergenerational retreat center was in fact the summer of 1963, when Carroll Hinderlie, undeniably the chief sculptor for molding the Holden we know today, took charge as first permanent director. Or, some might even contend that at least the conception of the Lutheran Holden happened in 1957, when a hopeful Wes Prieb wrote his first letter to Howe Sound asking about the property. (The buildings, it could be noted, celebrated their 50th birthday in 1987, and that year marked the centennial of Great Northern Railway's exploration of what came to be called Railroad Creek Valley.)

No matter how you date it, Holden as a Christian renewal center in 1987 was approaching the end of its first decade. And that was old enough to have a lot of story to be told.

The book is based on certain written records (see bibliography), but more particularly on the recollections of many who have been the shapers and beneficiaries of the Village. I benefited both from personal interviews with these people and from listening to their reflections via the oral history tapes that are available in the Village library. In all, I was privileged to have the reflections of more than 40 people available as background for the book. Special help was given by Bill Dierks, Holden historian/archivist.

## Family Enjoyment

My own experience with Holden began in the spring of 1960 when, as an editor in a Lutheran national youth office, I heard the hard-to-believe story of the gift of a complete mining village in the Cascades of Washington state. Over the next few years I helped tell the story of the Village's development in *One,* a youth magazine of The American Lutheran Church and the Augustana Lutheran Church.

I first visited the Village in the summer of 1965. Since then I have returned and served as a teaching staff member six more times in various June-to-September periods, and have paid one

February visit to the Village. I am married to Hertha, a Holden board member since 1983. Our family, including son Tim, daughter Gretchen, and son Nathan, has enjoyed Holden together on various occasions. Tim served six months as a Village carpenter in 1980.

While the book has been commissioned and published by Holden Village, any opinions not otherwise attributed are solely those of the author.

Charles P. Lutz<br>
Minneapolis

# 1 The Gift That Is Holden

*Sometimes I felt it was a shame that God gave a gift like this to God's least imaginative people—the Lutherans!*
*—Carroll L. Hinderlie, director of Holden Village, 1963-77*

Holden Village is a place of great physical beauty. It is 400 or more people gathered for celebration and learning. It is a facility that is unexpectedly comfortable, given its remoteness, while simultaneously offering opportunity for outdoor activity of intense rigor.

But more than anything else Holden is a gift. It came to the Lutherans as a gift, totally unexpected. It is only because of the extraordinary gift of labor by hundreds of volunteers each year that it is able to operate as a modestly priced center for families. Guests give of themselves also, in many ways. The Village continues to be a gift blessing those who go there. And its motivating energy from the start has been the Gospel, the story of divine giving, unearned and unconditional, to humankind.

Most assuredly, an important part of Holden's specialness is its physical remoteness. To put it simply, you can't drive your car there! For most North Americans, that fact alone makes a place at least unusual, probably suspect, even a bit unsettling. Holden is not easy to reach. You can hike in; while that takes several days, there are some who do it. You can take a float plane from Chelan to Lucerne and then hike or ride a bus the 11 miles to Holden. Or you can take a Lake Chelan boat for 2½ to 3½ hours (depending on where you board), then ride a bus for 40 minutes—the way the vast majority of summer Villagers get there.

## Rebirth Through the Water

This journey of about four hours is a decompression time for most. The trip itself enforces a transition from one pace to another, from one psyche to another. We move from our normal social settings, with their impersonal relationships, to one of intimacy and community, where all we have for a time is each other.

George Utech, a Lutheran poet-theologian, likened the long Lake Chelan boat trip to our baptism: "We are reborn, subconsciously prepared for a new life by that journey through the water!"

From Holden, communication with the rest of the world is difficult. There is radio connection with the outside via a Forest Service office in Chelan, a county sheriff's office in Stehekin, and a 911 emergency number in Chelan. But there is no telephone and no television in the Village, and broadcast radio reception is not good. Daily newspapers arrive by boat and bus a day or two late. People joke that the world could come to an end and Holden wouldn't know it for at least 24 hours. Once you're there, Holden seems to become the whole world, the only world there is.

And yet, in an ironic twist, perhaps because of the absence of our standard distractions, Holden Village for most participants is also an experience of being thrust into the ultimate questions of life and living. Reality is reduced to the basics, stripped of the clutter of non-essentials. The world and its needs are very much present in the Village, and its program and people from the beginning have been immersed in that larger world. So, while for many Holden is a retreat, it is certainly not an escape from the world into some idyllic or utopian hideaway. It is, supremely, a place where God's Good News is able to permeate the whole of human existence and experience.

It is difficult to capture the magic of Holden with words, for someone who has not been there. Listen to the kinds of comments you get when you ask Holdenites to try:

"Holden isn't so much a place as an experience."

"I can't explain its special hold on me—you'll have to go and see for yourself."

## The People Who Come

Who are these people who go to Holden Village? During the course of a year Holden will be host to some 5,500-6,000 individuals, counting all family members of guests and staff, short-term and long-term. About 80% of them come in the summer, which in program terms means June through September. Holden is near capacity every week from around mid-June to the end of August. September sees a rather full Village also, though without many school-age children.

From October to May the character of the Village community changes. The permanent population drops to 50 or 60, swelled on occasion by groups to a few hundred. (See Chapter Five.)

So most of the 6,000 know the Village only from its June-September face. The usual stay for a guest in the summer is one week, though others may register for shorter or longer periods. Short-term staff are expected to volunteer for a minimum of three weeks. Teaching staff typically stay for two or three weeks, sometimes longer and maybe an entire summer. Counting everybody, on a normal July or August day there will be 400 women, men, and children in the Village. It's likely that 240 of them will be paying guests and 160 will be staff (family members included). Roughly, that 60/40 ratio holds throughout the summer.

Until the end of August, as many as 80 or 90 of the 400 will be children and youth, from infants through high-school age. Holden is a family place, and that's one of the reasons it works. More will be said later about its family character.

The Village can comfortably care for around 400 people, and can crowd in 430 or so. (When it was a mining village, the normal population was 600-700, but in those days existed some 100 single family homes, destroyed in the fall of 1962.) There have been as many as 550 in the present Village on occasion for a day or two, but there aren't beds for that number so the extras will be in sleeping bags on the floor or outdoors.

The reason as many as 40% of the Village community needs to be staff (including family members) is that to function Holden must itself provide all the services that any small town would demand. That means not just accommodations and food, but also its own waste disposal, water supply and electricity, transportation to and from Lake Chelan and maintenance of 11 miles of mountain road, fire protection, care and repair of 30-plus buildings, health services, managing a store and snack bar, a post office, and even a 400-car parking facility down the lake. There is also a K-12 public school for the winter community families, a part of Lake Chelan School District No. 129, with two teachers and usually from six to 15 students.

The only reason Holden can exist in its present shape, with attractive rates allowing middle-income families to come, is the presence of this large staff of volunteers, whose free labor in fact is subsidizing every guest's stay. All volunteers, including teachers, receive only room and food and the opportunity to enjoy the Holden program and community—and that's all. They must even manage their own transportation to and from the Village.

Gifts from friends of the Village provide another part of its operating budget, which is currently about $1,000,000 a year, counting the time of volunteers at minimum wage equivalent. Overall, guests pay approximately 75% of what it costs the Village to receive them. (Chapter Six discusses the centrality of volunteerism at Holden.)

## Where They Are From

The geographic origins of the Holden community have remained fairly constant from the first years to the present. Its natural constituency lives in a right-angular configuration from Washington state south to California and east to Wisconsin and Illinois. About half the guests come from Washington. Three-fourths of the rest are from Minnesota, Oregon, and California. In recent years, among 4,000 annual guests, roughly 2,000 have come from Washington, 600 from Minnesota, 500 from Oregon, and 400 from California. In the summer months the proportion from Minnesota and other Midwest states is a bit higher than the rest of the year. Ten states—Washington, Oregon, California, Montana, the two Dakotas, Minnesota, Iowa, Wisconsin, and Illinois—account for almost 95% of the guests. A few Canadians, nearly all from British Columbia, are present every year, and a handful of overseas people find their way to the Village. Staff tend to come from the same places as guests, in about the same proportions.

Though records by church affiliation are not kept, it is a reliable guess that a large majority of Holdenites are Lutheran. It is also painfully evident that the Holden community is overwhelmingly white and middle class, even more than is true of its basic Lutheran constituency. Holden's leadership has considered its lack of diversity in race (and economic class) a serious problem for at least two decades and is still seeking significant ways of changing it. For the summer of 1987 a two-week program especially oriented to Black Americans was offered. Special guest leaders for "Rainbow on the Mountain-top" included Bishop Will Herzfeld of the Association of Evangelical Lutheran Churches and Dr. Pete Pero of the Lutheran School of Theology at Chicago.

People of all ages come to Holden. That's not according to the original plan, which envisioned Holden as primarily a center for young adults. But it soon evolved into a family place, which it remains each June through August. September has become a month chiefly for senior adults. The winter community is made up of families of staff and of an occasional sabbatical-taker, plus those (often single young adults) who are winter program participants and, in January, a college class on an interim month.

Holdenites tend to be physically fit, and the Village has been made as physically accessible as is possible in mountain terrain. Those with very technical medical needs are urged not to risk a visit. The reason, of course, is Holden's isolation. While it normally has a nurse on staff, in a major medical emergency an evacuation must be made by boat, float plane, or helicopter. When emergencies have happened, people have usually been delivered to medical care in less than two hours.

## What the Village Wants To Do

Why does a place known as Holden Village exist? The formal, purposeful reason is expressed in the Articles of Incorporation, as amended June 1984:

> Holden Village is organized to provide a community for healing, renewal, and refreshment of people through worship, intercession, study, humor, work, recreation, and conversation in a climate of mutual acceptance under the Lordship of Jesus Christ. The purpose of this community is to participate in the renewal of the church and the world by proclaiming the gospel of God's unconditional love in Jesus Christ; rehabilitating and equiping people for ministry in the world; lifting up a vision of God's

kingdom of peace, justice, and wholeness; and celebrating the unity and the diversity of the church, all humanity, and all creation.

Why does Holden Village exist? The historical and functional answer is that Holden exists because there were copper and other useful minerals in a mountain there, because a mining company assembled the capital and the people to remove them from the mountain, and because when the world price of copper declined in the late 1950s and the company quit mining a young man named Prieb wrote the company to ask about the property and eventually the company decided to give it to Prieb's church.

Which is to say that the Lutherans worked many years to refine the purpose and program of Holden Village, but they inherited the physical facility first and all at once, as a gift of pure grace.

Mary Hinderlie recalls how people "would speculate that maybe this retreat center is what God had in mind all along in permitting a mine to develop here." Her husband Carroll, Holden director from 1963 to 1977, liked to describe Holden as "a place for adults, especially, to have serious conversation, to bring their questions—not so much to find answers as to get a better quality of questions. And to have fun while doing it."

## Holden's "Holy Hilarity"

Fun is a central element in the Holden mix. Elmer Witt, director of the Village since 1984, likes to note that "Holden is no doubt one of the very few church-related organizations with the word *humor* in its articles of incorporation."

Humor has been important at the Village from its beginnings, and Carroll Hinderlie made certain that Holden and hilarity would be forever linked. There is a playfulness about all serious endeavor at Holden. Or, as some would prefer, being playful is serious business at Holden. "Holy hilarity" it has often been called. What it means is that at Holden neither people nor the Village itself can ever be taken too seriously.

But Hinderlie confesses that when he first heard of the mining village gift he "felt it was a mistake for the church to accept it. I thought it was just too remote from Lutheran strength areas."

Many of those responsible for making the initial decision about the gift property had similar thoughts.

Gil Berg, the Seattle businessman who was Holden's initial champion and enthusiastic manager its first three years as a Lutheran entity, said he was sold on the property from the first look. But, Gil recalls, "Many people felt that the big question facing us in those early years was whether it would be too isolated, too difficult for people to get there. Others wondered if it would prove too costly for a non-profit management to maintain."

Gil adds, "I felt it was precisely its isolation that would make it go. The remoteness would make it unique and appealing to people."

Hinderlie later came to hold the same view. "Our tremendous advantage from the beginning was our dramatic location, which had also seemed to some of us to be Holden's chief disadvantage."

Carroll's main worry at the outset was whether a rather conventional church people, not noted for taking risks or for daring the unusual, would ever support a vision of a retreat center in an isolated setting. As he puts it, "I felt it was a shame that God gave a gift like this to God's least imaginative people— the Lutherans!"

The fact was that, through a totally unplanned set of developments, these unimaginative Lutherans found they had dropped in their laps a magnificent physical facility in a breathtaking mountain setting . . . and now they needed to fashion a program that would do it justice. But what sort of program, for which kinds of people? And who should be in charge? In answering such questions it became clear that even Lutherans have quite a few imaginative and creative folks.

## What Does God Have in Mind?

Usually, of course, new ideas in the church's mission unfold the other way around—from a vision to a program and only then, if it's needed, to developing a physical facility to fit. Thus, while lots of people were excited about the property and the setting, no one was quite comfortable with the kind of challenge this old mining village represented. There was no early agreement on what it was that God had in mind. But a fair number of people were certain that it was indeed a gift from God that should be used for God's purposes, whatever they proved to be.

Everyone seemed to agree that the church didn't need another Bible camp. There was also early consensus that the constituency ought to be continental, not regional, in scope. Those who had early custody of the gift turned almost immediately to the national church bodies, and the focus went to the youth boards of those churches.

The gift had initially been received by Lutheran Bible Institute (LBI) of Seattle in May 1960 (details will be shared in Chapter Three). LBI was the recipient because Wes Prieb, who on his own had written to Howe Sound three times, asking about the availability of the property, was a student there when two of his letters were sent. The company would make the gift only to a responsible organization, not to an individual. LBI had immediate interest in the possibilities and for a time flirted with the idea of operating the Village. And it was LBI staff and board members who provided the early leadership. But before long LBI people recognized that the project was more than their institution could manage.

There was some early interest by the Lutheran Council of Seattle and the Lutheran jurisdictions of the Northwest were consulted. But all the signals indicated clearly that national church involvement would be advisable. Within a few months the youth leadership of the just-forming American Lutheran Church, the soon-to-be-formed Lutheran Church in America, and the Lutheran Church—Missouri Synod were invited into the Holden picture. It was a time when youth ministry in Lutheran bodies was identified with church renewal, theological excitement, societal engagement, and risk-taking.

## Vital Support from Youth Boards

It was a fortuitous mix. The youth boards gave Holden much of its early financial support and program direction as well as national church identity that was vital to its future. The shaping of Holden as a place of creativity and renewal can also be attributed to the youth leaders who were involved from near the beginning. Thus, the early commitment of the national Lutheran youth departments was crucial.

And yet, Holden has evolved as a center for families and adults, not as the early vision had it: a place for ministry with young adults and youth leaders. What happened?

In order to trace the story of Holden's development we need to turn back to the beginning, and tell in more detail how a mining village came to be in the Railroad Creek Valley and how it happened to come as a gift to the Lutherans.

# 2 Holden—The Man and His Mine

*The Holden mine became Washington state's largest copper, gold, and zinc mine and remained so until it was closed in 1957. The mine . . . left abundant evidence to industrialists and conservationists that the mineral resources of the Cascade Mountains were as exploitable as the scenery.*
—*Nigel B. Adams, Holden mine historian**

Rudy Edmund, Holden geologist, believes that the last glacier in Railroad Creek Valley melted about 10,000 years ago. That glacier, feeding into the ice mass which was carving the Lake Chelan trough, left behind a U-shaped valley and an exposed portion of copper-bearing ore. Those ancient glaciers are important to Holden Village today because they left a long, navigable lake and a gentle, inhabitable valley. They afforded access to human beings who wished to come and look for minerals in the nearby mountains and, finding them, to organize a human settlement devoted to their extraction. Without a glacier-carved lake and valley, there most likely would not have been a mine, and without the mine there most surely would not be a Holden Village today.

While native Americans spent time along the shores of Lake Chelan, there is no evidence that they ever settled permanently

---

\* This chapter draws heavily from Adams' *The Holden Mine: Discovery to Production, 1896-1938* (Washington State Historical Society, 1981) and from Rudolph W. Edmund's *The Mine* (Holden Village Press).

in the Railroad Creek Valley. Exploration by Europeans in the North Cascades and around the northern part of Lake Chelan was extensive from the late 1870s. Both the Northern Pacific and Great Northern railroads explored possible rail routes through the Northern Cascades by way of Railroad Creek Valley.

Taking minerals from a remote wilderness area like the Northern Cascades is no simple enterprise. One mine on the western slope, Monte Cristo, some 30 miles southwest of Holden, did operate profitably from 1892 to 1909. Nigel B. Adams, historian of the Holden mine, reports that Monte Cristo was developed with $3,000,000 of primarily Rockefeller money and produced approximately $7,000,000 in gold and silver. Adams writes in *The Holden Mine: Discovery to Production, 1896-1938:*

> The Monte Cristo discovery raised hopes for similar rewards in the upper Chelan area, where there had been scattered prospecting since the late 1870s. Once most of the Monte Cristo area had been staked and claimed, attention shifted northward to the Skagit River region and then to the Stehekin River valley, which emptied into the northern end of Lake Chelan. By August 1891 miners established the Lake Chelan Mining District in order to regulate filing and transfers of claims, and to resolve conflicts.

## Who Was J. H. Holden?

James Henry Holden came to the Lake Chelan area in 1893, seeking ore that could be mined. Holden had been born in Springfield, Massachusetts, in 1855 and had come west in 1874 after growing up in New York state. He worked for a time in the mines at Virginia City, Nevada, and as an ore inspector at a smelter near Denver. Investing in unprofitable claims in Colorado left him penniless. He moved to the Seattle area where, in 1888, he met Victor Denny, member of a family with mining and real estate interests. Holden was employed by the Denny family part-time during the next five years, and he and Victor became close friends. (The "Denny" perpetuated in Seattle place names to this day commemorates this family.)

In July of 1893 the Dennys hired Holden to go to Lake Chelan, prepare for a family camping trip, and do some prospecting. After making the camping trip preparations, Holden traveled up Lake Chelan to explore mining prospects. Holden returned to the Puget Sound area that fall, but was back prospecting in the Lake Chelan area in 1894 and 1895, living on income from part-time jobs and on loans from the Dennys.

Holden staked no claims from these expeditions but he remained confident. With Victor Denny he planned another prospecting trip for the spring of 1896. They spent April and early May exploring the shoreline of upper Lake Chelan, until Denny was called home by the family. Now Holden alone began to explore Railroad Creek Valley. In mid-July he hired a W. P. Robinson to help him pack supplies 15 miles up Railroad Creek, to a point not far below Hart Lake. Adams reports that Robinson later recalled Holden saying he was ready to quit prospecting and work as a ranch-hand for the Dennys if this trip produced no claim.

After moving his operation three miles down the valley, on July 24, 1896, Holden noticed a promising outcropping of ore up the side of what we now know as Copper Mountain, about 1500 feet above the creek. Holden investigated immediately and decided he had discovered a substantial body of ore. The assayer report confirmed that Holden did indeed have a major copper find.

Adams observes that "Holden's conduct after his discovery was far from exemplary. He made promises easily before the discovery but later found reasons not to keep his word."

It became clear that Holden intended to keep his find entirely for himself. He had earlier told the packer Robinson that if they discovered ore "you shall be in it with me." But after the discovery Robinson was denied any share. Further, he excluded the Denny family from any partnership in the mine, even though they had kept him going with loans and his friend Victor had been along at the beginning of the 1896 prospecting trip.

(The Denny family later sued Holden for the right to participate in his claim, but lost on a court decision in the early 1900s.)

Thus J. H. Holden, at age 41, found himself the possessor of a rich mineral deposit with "all the earmarks of one of the greatest mines in existence" (said a mining consultant for the Great Northern in 1898). But Holden had no money to develop his claim. His find would not become a producing mine for another 42 years, 20 years after his death, though it would furnish a stable income for Holden and his family because of funds provided by various investors who saw the mine's potential.

## One of Chelan's First Citizens

At first Holden had little luck finding investment funds to allow development of the mine. Adams notes that the discovery received fine publicity and many visitors, but "nobody appeared ready to invest." During these years Holden also settled in Chelan and started a family—in 1898 he married Alma Lord, a local rancher's daughter who was 20 years his junior; the first of their four sons was born in 1899.

Finally in October 1899, Holden formed the Holden Gold and Copper Mining Company, with main office in Chelan. From sale of stock Holden raised enough to be able to hire a crew. Tunneling into Copper Mountain began immediately and by the fall of 1901 buildings were ready to house a foreman and a dozen workers. The tailings produced by this early work are still clearly visible from the Village as three rust-colored scars high on the face of Copper Mountain.

Though Holden continued working at it, the mine's development was stalled by lack of money and by the unsolved major question: how to move the ore from the mine to Chelan? No breakthrough had come by the time Holden died of cancer, at age 63, on May 19, 1918.

But if Holden did not live to see a producing mine, he had certainly acquired a good living and social acceptance for himself and his family in Chelan. At his death he was owner of not only a copper mine up the lake but also of 13 Chelan city lots. From his Irish Catholic background he had moved to active involvement in St. Andrew Episcopal Church, where his wife Alma was Sunday school superintendent for many years. In 1904 Holden moved his aging parents from Iowa to live with him in Chelan. A brother also came west to work for Holden, but a sister remained behind in Sac City, Iowa.

Holden and Alma both had a major interest in music. She sang and played piano while he played cornet and other brass instruments. He also helped to organize a community band in Chelan. But generally Holden kept a low profile in Chelan affairs. Adams observes that Holden "occasionally performed as a responsible community leader of quiet influence, when he was not preoccupied with promoting the mine and supervising property developments uplake."

The Holdens' son Harold (born 1899) became a composer and musical director for Twentieth Century Fox motion pictures. Charles (born 1905) became a marine engineer and plant manager. Lucian (born 1909) sang professionally and drove trucks. William (born 1917) became a golf professional. Alma Holden lived mostly in the Chelan area until her death at age 89 in 1964.

## Enter Howe Sound Mining Company

After the death of J. H. Holden, a Chelan apple grower and banker named Crooker Perry promoted the mine successfully, eventually selling it to the Howe Sound Mining Company. Perry had little interest in mining copper. But he had made a loan to Holden in 1915; in order to recover it he became directly involved in the company in the 1920s. While Alma Holden continued to hold a major interest, Perry became president and reorganized the company as Lake Chelan Copper Company.

Howe Sound had been mining copper since 1905. It was headquartered at Britannia Beach on Howe Sound in British Columbia, 20 miles north of Vancouver (its main office was later moved to New York City). In November 1930 Howe Sound agreed to buy the claims and assets of the Lake Chelan Copper Company for just under $250,000. A much relieved Crooker Perry then had the task of locating and settling with all of Holden's investors. Adams reports that Perry found 49 such shareholders or their immediate relatives and gave "careful, sensitive, but sometimes routine and monotonous explanations to impatient people caught in the Depression."

Howe Sound had taken a lease on the Holden mine already in 1928 and from then until the end of 1931 it explored the ore deposit quite extensively and began construction of a main tunnel. It had a work force of more than 100, who lived in the area now known as "Honeymoon Heights." Howe Sound even applied for a fourth-class post office to be designated "Chelcop" (for Chelan Copper). But the Depression and low copper prices forced a work suspension in December 1931.

The company also faced environmental problems during these early years. There was opposition from several state agencies, from sports groups in Chelan and Wenatchee, and from members of the public. Much of the concern focused on the pollution of Railroad Creek and Lake Chelan that could result from mine tailings. The state game commission finally agreed to the company's proposals for protecting the environment. But the fears of opponents, as Adams notes, "were to be confirmed when after only two months of production beginning in 1938 the tailings dike broke, making the water between the mine and [Lake Chelan] unsafe to drink. However, the state took no action to stop the mining."

The mining company also had to solve the problems of transportation to and from Lake Chelan and of electrical power for the mine and the community that would live there. The former was addressed by building a road of nearly 11 miles, with switchbacks rising some 1,200 feet in the first mile. For power, the company wanted to develop a hydroelectric plant at the outlet of Domke Lake. When both the state and the U.S. Forest Service refused to approve this plan, Howe Sound gained permission to build a 54-mile power line to the Washington Water Power Company's Chelan Falls station.

In 1936 Howe Sound decided to complete the mine's haulage tunnel and in 1937 it began construction of the surface facilities needed to bring a mine into operation: a mill, concentrating plant, docks on Lake Chelan, shop buildings and offices, assay facilities, and living accommodations for the miners and their families.

## Holden Town Is Built

The community, earlier labeled Chelcop, was to be called Holden. Apparently there was no debate over the name, since the site had been known locally as "the Holden mine" for four decades. Provision for at least 450 people was called for. (The original accommodations near the mine on the south side of Railroad Creek could handle only about 100.) As townsite Howe Sound selected a recessional moraine north of the creek. A recessional moraine is an "irregular deposit of unsorted rock left by the retreating ice mass" of a glacier (Edmund). Timber was cut from the townsite and nearby, and additional lumber was bought from a Manson mill.

Six 50-person dormitories, 10 family homes and one guest house (the chalets—three more were built later), a 264-person dining hall, recreation hall (today's Village Center), hospital, school, and staff house for single engineers and managers were all completed between 1937 and 1940.

When some workers asked for more family housing, a residential area west of the main townsite was built by Winston Brothers (and thus often called "Winston Camp"). Some 100 small homes were eventually built (they all were burned by the Forest Service in the fall of 1962). Adams says this development "separated the community geographically and socially . . . [with] single workers and management in the main part of town and most of the working class families in the residential addition."

Because the mine and the town were located inside Wenatchee National Forest, all construction had to meet specifications of the U.S. Forest Service. Fire safety was another major concern. While there was loss of life from one home fire in Winston Camp, and some miners died of mine accidents, the mine itself never had a serious fire. Rudy Edmund notes in his: *The Mine: Holden Village* that "the safety record of the company was excellent."

The arrival of the first concentrate at the company dock in Chelan on April 9, 1938, was cause for region-wide rejoicing. Businesses and schools in Chelan closed for the ceremonies, the high school band played, and area dignitaries made speeches about the significance of the mine's opening. Following the speeches, everybody hopped into cars and paraded after the first truckload of concentrate through town to Chelan Falls, where it was loaded on a rail car for shipment to the smelter in Tacoma. Adams notes that the speeches and newspaper reports, which gave high honor to Crooker Perry, made no mention of "the importance of the mine's discoverer, J. H. Holden."

## $66 Million in Metals

That first truckload of concentrate was followed by many more during the ensuing 19 years. Adams reports that 212,000,000 pounds of copper, 40,000,000 pounds of zinc, 2,000,000 ounces of silver, and 600,000 ounces of gold were extracted from 10,000,000 tons of ore. The gross value of those metals was $66,000,000. It was, says Adams, "the largest non-ferrous mine in Washington state."

The excavation inside Copper Mountain was extensive. If we were able to enter the mine today we would find 56 miles of tunnels, most at one time lined with railroad track. The tunnels and vertical shafts connect vast and deep cavities left by the extraction of rock and mineral, some of them large enough to absorb all of the Holden townsite. From the mine entrance at 3500 feet above sea level (about 300 feet above the Village main street), the ore body was mined both up and down, about a half-mile top to bottom. Horizontally, the tunnels slice into Copper Mountain for some 2500 feet along the ore body, all connected to a single tunnel that served as the main entrance. The ore body itself was about 80 feet thick.

Edmund writes that the copper, zinc, silver, and gold came comingled, were contained in very hard crystalline rock, and had to be removed mechanically. He describes that process as follows:

> [It] involved breaking down both rock and mineral to almost a powder, then separating the ore from the waste rock by flotation. The lighter rock material was then moved by water as tailings, piled along Railroad Creek below the mine, and the minerals concentrated for the smelting and refining process. The mineral concentrates were dried and placed in large pail-shaped metal containers, each holding approximately five tons of concentrate. These containers were lifted on trucks by large cranes and hauled to the dock at Lucerne where they were transferred by crane to the barges on Lake Chelan. The barges delivered the ore to the

city of Chelan, 40 miles south. Trucks moved the ore 12 miles to the railroad at Chelan Station for its final 225-mile journey to the smelter at Tacoma. The long haul from the inaccessible mine to the smelter, almost 300 miles, always constituted an unfavorable economic factor in competition with other copper mines.

## Why the Mine Closed

Still, Holden Mine was profitable, partly because U.S. government policies through World War II and the Korean War encouraged domestic mining of copper. Howe Sound was even able to get a tax credit in 1954 to pay for half of its efforts (unsuccessful) to locate other ore bodies in Buckskin Mountain or to the northwest toward Bonanza Mountain. During the 1954-57 period the U.S. government bought half of the copper produced at Holden for 32 cents a pound. In 1956 the world price peaked at 46 cents, but then it fell to 24 cents in early 1957 and Howe Sound decided to quit at Holden.

Not only was the price trend downward, but by 1957 the easily reached ore had been significantly depleted (the ore available then was being lifted 1000 feet to the main tunnel), the capital equipment was wearing out, labor and transportation costs were rising, and the company's 20-year tax depletion allowance would expire in August of that year. There were sound economic reasons for discontinuing.

The community had heard rumors, but the February 1957 announcement that the mine would close by July 1 still came as a surprise to most of the Holden people. Many had lived there for 20 years; some of the children knew no other home. (Nigel Adams, the mine historian, was taken to Holden by his parents at the age of two months in 1939 and lived there, when not attending local high school, until the mine closed 18 years later.) For most of the original Holden residents, it had been a very pleasant home, indeed.

It was a company town, but not in the traditional sense. The miners were unionized, the pay was good, and the amenities were attractive. It benefited from progressive Canadian and U.S. corporate management. "The people of the community initiated a great deal of social and economic betterment themselves," says Adams.

During most of the 20 years, 1937-57, Holden employed 350 to 400 persons. The town population was normally around 600. The mine operated five days a week on a 24-hour basis, with three eight-hour shifts.

In the early years the company allowed no private businesses, but salesmen were permitted to visit the town and families could order groceries from a Chelan store and other merchandise by mail. Later the company contracted with a private business to run the well-stocked grocery and allowed a blinded miner to run a general hardware store. Adams writes of the community's monetary system, created because Holden had no bank:

> The company made tin 50-cent pieces, packaged in $5 packages, and employees or their spouses signed receipts at the commissary when they wanted money. The payroll office then deducted the amounts from the employee's wages.

The company originally permitted no liquor store on the premises, hoping thereby to reduce absenteeism and increase productivity. Liquor orders for home consumption could be given to the bus driver who traveled daily between Holden and Lucerne. Later a package store operated in the space now occupied by Koinonia's fireplace room. A town constable enforced county and state laws.

The town was granted its own school district, named Howe Sound School District No. 121, and employed up to five teachers for as many as 100 students in grades one through eight.

A private kindergarten was operated. For high school, Holden youth went to Chelan or another outside community.

The lower floor of Lodge Six contained the Peter Rabbit Grocery Store. The present Shaft in the Village Center was a card-playing room and the pool hall office housed the mine cashier. Today's kitchen and dining room served the same purpose in mining days. A variety store and post office were in the location of the present bookstore and post office.

Chalet One housed the families of the mine superintendents: John J. Curzon (1937-54) and Daniel J. Roper (1954-57). Other mine executive families occupied the remaining chalets, while single miners lived in the lodges and other families in Winston Camp west of the main townsite.

## No Permanent Clergy Allowed

Organized religious life was controlled by the company. Howe Sound felt that in so small a community the organizing of competing congregations might be disruptive. So it did not allow resident paid clergy, but visiting ministers and priests were welcomed on a rotating basis to provide a monthly service. Resident lay people also conducted non-denominational services and Sunday school, and were available to provide comfort to injured miners.

Rudy Edmund reports that the gymnasium (now the Village Center) was "a place of much enjoyable activity and entertainment." There were movies every Wednesday, Friday, and Sunday night, and a series of basketball games every winter. On holidays, dance orchestras and other forms of entertainment were featured, funded by a monthly $5 deduction from paychecks. A TV antenna was put high on Copper Mountain and television was piped into the recreation hall. There was a bowling alley and pool hall in the basement of that building, and they continue to serve Villagers 30 years later. Former residents

**HOLDEN AND HIS MINE.** J. H. Holden in his 20s (left—photo courtesy of Holden family) and in his 50s (photo by Wenatchee Daily World). BELOW: Holden mill in late 1930s with Buckskin Mountain as backdrop (photo by Larry Penberthy, a chemist with Howe Sound Company).

**ORE MOVEMENT.** This sketch of mine and mill was done in the early 1950s by F. H. Brogan.

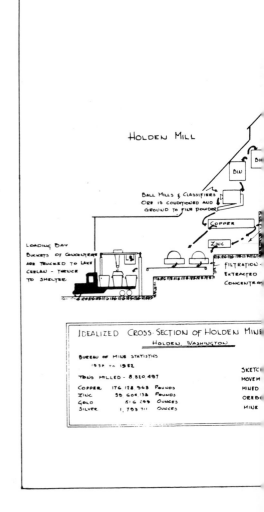

HOLDEN MILL

BIN

BIN

BALL MILLS & CLASSIFIERS
ORE IS CONDITIONED AND
GROUND TO FINE POWDER

COPPER

ZINC

LOADING BAY
BUCKETS OF CONCENTRATE
ARE TRUCKED TO LAKE
CHELAN - THENCE
TO SMELTER

FILTRATION -
EXTRACTED
CONCENTRATE

IDEALIZED CROSS-SECTION OF HOLDEN MINE
HOLDEN, WASHINGTON

BUREAU OF MINE STATISTICS
1938 TO 1952

TONS MILLED - 8,820,497

| COPPER | 176,128,568 | POUNDS |
| ZINC | 58,604,138 | POUNDS |
| GOLD | 516,209 | OUNCES |
| SILVER | 1,793,711 | OUNCES |

SKETCH
MOVEM
MINED
ORE BO
MINE

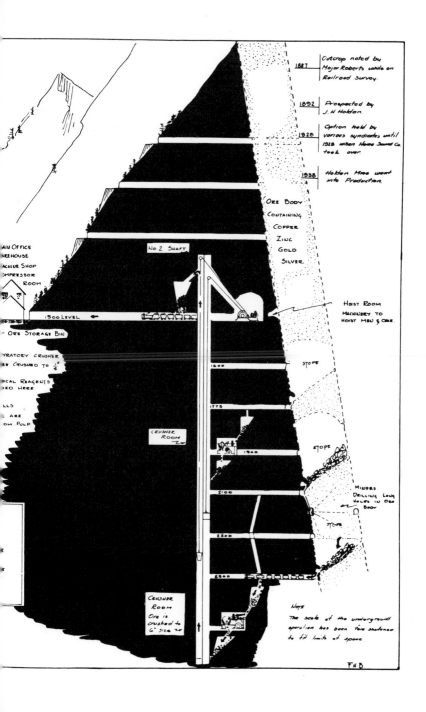

1887  Outcrop noted by Major Roberts while on Railroad Survey.

1892  Prospected by J. H. Holden

1928  Option held by various syndicates until 1928 when Howe Sound Co. took over.

1938  Holden Mine went into Production.

ORE BODY
CONTAINING
COPPER
ZINC
GOLD
SILVER

No 2 Shaft

MAIN OFFICE
WAREHOUSE
MACHINE SHOP
COMPRESSOR ROOM

HOIST ROOM
MACHINERY TO HOIST MEN & ORE

1500 LEVEL

ORE STORAGE BIN

1600  STOPE

GYRATORY CRUSHER
ORE CRUSHED TO 1¼"

1775

CHEMICAL REAGENTS
ADDED HERE

1900  STOPE

CRUSHER ROOM

BALLS
ORE ARE
FROM PULP

2100  MINERS DRILLING LONG HOLES IN ORE BODY

2300  STOPE

2500

CRUSHER ROOM
Ore is crushed to 6" Size

NOTE
The scale of the underground operation has been fore shortened to fit limits of space

F.H.B

**WINSTON CAMP** (foreground) and mill (center background) in winter (photo from Nigel B. Adams collection). BELOW: Trucks with canisters, each holding five tons of concentrate, ready for trip to Lucerne dock in late 1930s (Penberthy photo).

recall that in the 1940s a young actress named Elizabeth Taylor performed on the stage of the recreation hall.

Winters for the mining community were long and the snow was deep. Official records indicate that the highest snowfall—640 inches—fell at the townsite in 1955-56, when one could walk out second-story windows on top of the snow. The snow provided fine recreational opportunities. On two occasions people constructed ski lifts on a slope near the lower edge of Martin Ridge at the west end of the miners' village. Rudy Edmund notes that probably "no mining village was ever situated in an area more favorable for fishing in the summertime and hunting in the wintertime."

By the testimony of those who lived there, Holden in its mining days was a happy place to live and work. Many of the mining families still like to visit, bringing children and grandchildren to see their former mountain home.

When Holden Village in the summer of 1977 hosted a celebration of the 20th anniversary of the mine's closing, some 230 former residents assembled for a day (and another 150 came to commemorate the 25th anniversary in 1982). The 1977 group placed on a wall in the Village Center a plaque (now located on the north wall of the Portal Museum) with the following inscription:

### The Holden Mine (1896-1957)

*In memory of the many people who were associated with the discovery, mining, managing, engineering, milling and transporting of the ore of the largest known low-grade copper deposit in the Cascades.*

*Here people proved that mineral deposits could be removed from the remote regions of the Cascades, and that damage to the scenic and recreational potential could be kept to a minimum.*

*Here people raised families, experienced a community life and enjoyed the outdoors.*

*When the mine closed in 1957 so did an important part of the history of the Lake Chelan region.*

*By the Lake Chelan Historical Society
and former residents of the Holden Mine*

# 3 The Village Goes To Church

*I really did not expect the company to give the property away, but I hoped they would reduce the price, or some miracle might happen.*
—*Wes Prieb, writer of letters asking Howe Sound Company about the mining village that was for sale*

As soon as the mine's closing was announced, people wondered what would happen to the facility. The external mine buildings could be sold for salvage of materials—and soon were—but what of the townsite and the miners' housing development? The Forest Service viewed abandoned buildings as a fire hazard and an attraction to vandals, and would not let them stand there unused for long.

Howe Sound immediately listed the townsite for sale as a mountain resort, with a real estate agency named Previews Incorporated, a national clearing house with West Coast offices in California. A large pictorial brochure was published presenting Holden as a "complete village, magnificently located in the Switzerland of America." It was advertised as having "splendid development potential for a large ski lodge, resort, corporation, or institution."

A few groups, both commercial and non-profit, did show interest. Private resort developers eventually concluded it would not be profitable. And nonprofit organizations (including the Boy Scouts of America and a Seattle area fire department) lacked the capital needed to make it functional. A particular problem was electrical power for the Village. The expensive transformer equipment at the mill had already been removed.

## Ghost Town Tours

Meanwhile, the Village immediately became a modest tourist attraction. The private resort at Lucerne on the lake promoted it as a "ghost town" and took visitors up and back for a fee.

Even before the mine was closed, Wes Prieb, a 34-year-old serving as a purchasing agent with the Army Corps of Engineers in Alaska, learned of Howe Sound's plan to cease operations. On a day in early June 1957, while waiting for a ride to a church picnic in Anchorage, Wes was paging through that day's *Anchorage Times*. He read that the Holden mine would close by the end of the month and that the townsite was for sale at $100,000. A product of Webster, South Dakota, Wes had never been to Holden. But upon reading about the complete mining village facility, it occurred to him that it might make a good church camp or retreat center.

On June 7, 1957, Wes wrote to the Holden mine manager to ask for more information. "I really did not expect the company to give the property away," Wes recalls, "but I hoped they would reduce the price, or some miracle might happen."

The mine superintendent, Daniel J. Roper, immediately replied saying the property was for sale at $100,000. (See appendices for full text of the Prieb letters and the Howe Sound replies.)

In April 1958 Wes wrote to Mr. Roper again, this time asking about the status of Holden and expressing the opinion that "this property would be ideal . . . as a . . . retreat center for the general use of the church and the Lutheran Bible Institute." By this time Wes was enrolled as a student at the Seattle LBI.

Daniel Roper's reply was the same as it had been 10 months earlier: "Holden Village is available for the price of $100,000."

Wes continued to think about the abandoned village. He waited two years, then in April of 1960 sent a third letter with the same request. Within a few weeks Wes received a telegram asking him to place a collect call to a Mr. A. G. Kirkland at Magnum, Utah.

"I made the call and was told that Howe Sound had decided to give the Holden property to LBI, on the condition that LBI send a statement saying it had received a gift in the amount of $100,000."

## A "Phony and Ridiculous" Offer

Most people had difficulty believing the offer when they first heard of it. LBI President E. V. Stime said later that the gift sounded "phony and a bit ridiculous."

There were other responses. One church official told Wes that "the Lutheran church doesn't need any more Bible camps." Another person said the place "should be turned over to the U.S. government and used as a center for the training of spies."

But the LBI people decided to give serious consideration to the offer. The first need was to take a look at the property. At the beginning of June 1960 a team of five LBI-related persons visited the Village. In the group were LBI President Stime, his son Randy, David Thorson (LBI business manager), Pastor Erman Lunder (an LBI faculty member), and Prieb (who had just finished his studies at LBI).

Pastor Stime commented some months later, "We haven't yet recovered from the shock of what we found." Lunder recalls that they were impressed with the property but saw many problems that would have to be resolved. He also remembers that

Randy Stime became an immediate promoter and was the one who enlisted the interest of Gil Berg, an LBI board member and Lutheran Free Church layman who owned a Seattle fuel oil business. The 61-year-old Berg made an appraisal trip to the Village, became an enthusiastic supporter of the venture, and soon emerged as leader of the feasibility committee.

"I had friends who had been engineers at the Holden mine and so had heard about the place," Gil recalls. "And I had visited Lucerne and Stehekin, but until June of 1960 I had never been to Holden itself."

An informal meeting was held at Berg's Seattle home on June 29, 1960. Soon thereafter Gil was named chair of a newly formed feasibility committee. That group agreed that another visit to Holden should be made soon by Berg and people with technical expertise.

Berg's group visited the Village for two days and spent their overnight on the living room floor of Chalet One (later to be named the Gil Berg Chalet). "I remember the place was crawling with mice and rats," says Berg. "Even before I fell asleep a rat came by and tried to drag my shoe over by the fireplace."

The group's main concern on this visit was the physical condition and accessibility of the Village—would people in large numbers be able to get there and then to live in relative comfort? They reported to the next meeting of the feasibility committee that water, sewer, lake transportation, dock at Lucerne, and the 11-mile road presented no serious problems. Electrical power, however, might be a big cost item.

They also shared highly positive responses from conversations with Forest Service officials in Wenatchee, who seemed eager to have a responsible church organization operating the Village. Finally, the group reported strong support from the Lutherans of Chelan and central and eastern Washington, and from the Chelan Chamber of Commerce.

## "The Village Was Walking Away"

A major concern was vandalism. The mining company had kept a small watchdog crew at the Village for about one year after the closing, but no such person had been there for the last two years. A contract had been given to a salvage company for removal of steel and other valuable materials from the mine buildings, and the salvagers were at work. The problem was that unauthorized salvagers were also at work—in the townsite. And vandalism, apparently by hikers passing through who would use and abuse the buildings, was serious.

Visitors on resort-sponsored trips also took items, and there was evidence that resort operators themselves were appropriating Village property. Sometime after the summer of 1960 a pack train came into the Village and took out many items of value, including about a thousand blankets.

"The Village was walking away," Berg recalls. "We simply had to get someone in there to watch over it."

At a meeting in July the feasibility committee agreed that placing a custodian at the Village was of the highest priority, and that an agreement should be reached with Howe Sound permitting that. But, as Luvern Rieke recalls, "Even the simple preservation of the property involved putting together a structure and raising money."

The feasibility committee had almost no money; a $200 grant from the Lutheran Council of Greater Seattle was welcome but would not last long. So raising funds became a priority. And some immediate physical repairs were necessary, before the next winter season. Snow had not been removed from roofs during the past three winters and that had caused some damage. Window panes were broken everywhere. It seemed to the committee that everything had to be done at once, and the committee had little authority or support for doing it.

Yet, most of those who visited Holden that summer of 1960 concluded that it had to be taken and used by the church in some way. Luvern Rieke: "My first reaction was to dream about all the wonderful things that could be done with this remarkable facility." Merton Strommen, one of the first national youth leaders to visit: "My immediate thought was that this would be an excellent gathering place for young adults." Gil Berg: "What sold me was that it was built very substantially; structurally, it was extremely solid."

The committee's report to LBI included two chief recommendations—that LBI should take the necessary legal steps for acceptance of the Holden property; that LBI should clarify its position regarding future sponsorship and ownership of the Village.

The LBI board accepted both recommendations at a special meeting on August 18, 1960. It also created an interim committee to act on Holden matters until a permanent sponsoring arrangement would be in place. Joining Berg and LBI President Stime on the interim committee were Bernard Anderson, Donald Compaan, Orion Davids, Earl Eckstrom, Emil Kallevig, Charles Moren, Eric Pihl, and Lawrence Puffert.

Randy Stime spent some time as a watchman at the Village during the latter part of the summer. The interim committee then arranged with Wes Prieb, who had spent the summer as a counselor at a Volunteers of America camp near Sultan, Washington, to go as watchman for most of September and October. Berg remembers that Wes put up signs around the Village saying, "The Lord punishes those who steal." Wes had finished his LBI course the previous June. From 1961 through most of the decade he worked in Indian mission programs in Alaska and Arizona. Wes began spending summers at Holden in 1969 and since 1970 has been director of the pool room every June through September.

The Village was empty of human presence the winter of 1960-61. Beginning with May 1961 a man named Rueben

Thompson was hired as full-time custodian and he spent the next two winters at the Village alone, with only his dog Bugger as companion.

While the LBI board had accepted the idea that it was feasible to operate the Village for church purposes, no one yet knew what the program ought to be. "We decided to wait with program discussion until more church leaders could have a chance to visit the site," said Berg. "I remember that one of our early plans was to bring all the district and synod presidents of the Lutheran bodies to the Village. That didn't happen, though we did get quite a few of them there early on."

## Youth Leaders Bring National Support

By December of 1960 several significant developments had occurred:

1. Negotiations with Howe Sound had been completed and legal documents were in preparation for receiving the gift of the property.

2. Fundraising and publicity about the Village were under way on a modest basis.

3. A permanent Holden board replaced the interim committee and Luvern Rieke, a University of Washington law professor, was chosen to chair it.

4. Gil Berg was called as executive director.

5. The youth departments of the national Lutheran churches were drawn into leadership and program development, and a statement of purpose was adopted in consultation with them. It specified that Holden Village should be "a Lutheran center where youth and adults interested in youth may find spiritual, intellectual, and physical renewal for Kingdom service."

It was agreed that the permanent Holden board would have its first meeting in May 1961, with major youth department representation included. Meanwhile, the interim committee continued to meet about once a month, in regular consultation with the youth offices.

Among the youth leaders who responded with great interest to the Holden possibility were:

*Merton Strommen,* director of Lutheran Youth Research and former youth director of the Lutheran Free Church. It was Strommen who took the lead in developing interest among the various Lutheran youth departments.

*Wilton Bergstrand,* youth director of the Augustana Lutheran Church, which was to become part of the Lutheran Church in America by 1963.

*L. David Brown,* youth director of The American Lutheran Church, which had just been constituted in the spring of 1960.

*Ewald (Joe) Bash* of Brown's staff, who had major early involvement with program development.

*Elmer Witt,* director of the Walther League, serving youth of the Lutheran Church—Missouri Synod.

*Calvin J. Storley,* newly named as youth director of the LFC, which would become part of The ALC in 1963.

And *Carroll Hinderlie.* Carroll was just completing his work as director of youth ministry in the Evangelical Lutheran Church, one of the partners in the new ALC, and would soon be teaching theology at Luther Seminary in St. Paul.

The interest and involvement of LBI continued. It had membership on the initial board that was organized in late 1960 and contributed to the program planning. Indeed, the only program offered the following summer, other than a work camp, was provided by LBI. Sessions for four groups were led between mid-July and mid-August by Pastor Erman Lunder of the LBI faculty. But LBI knew it did not want complete responsibility for Holden and graciously turned it over to others.

"Lutheran Bible Institute was very good about this entire operation," recalls Luvern Rieke, who had joined the feasibility committee in July of 1960 and then served as chair of the Village board from late 1960 until 1978. "From the beginning LBI did not want continuing responsibility for the Village but sought a separate corporation."

Another early question concerned the name of the enterprise. The mining town was usually called simply "Holden" but from the beginning the Lutherans felt something more descriptive was needed. In September 1960 the interim committee proposed "Holden Village in Luther Alps" as the name, and a few months later "Hidden Village" received serious consideration. By early 1961 "Holden Village" was being tried with various subtitles in an effort to identify it more fully. First it was "a Swiss village in the wilderness of the Northern Cascades"; then it became "an Alpine village in the wilderness of [etc.]." In May 1961 the new board settled on "Holden Village: A Place Apart" and that was used widely for a number of years. Eventually, as the Village and its program became widely known, there seemed little need for a descriptive subtitle and it has remained simply "Holden Village."

## Berg Becomes Key Man

Early in the spring of 1961 Gil Berg asked family members to manage his heating and electrical business and he moved to the Village to begin the work of restoration with volunteer help. "At first we didn't have a dime," Gil says. "Then a few hundred dollars was gathered. People would visit and become interested, giving us money or in-kind gifts. A new van was contributed by the Sheffels family, who were wheat farmers in eastern Washington. Many folks contributed labor."

In the spring and summer of 1962 and 1963 Lutheran ranchers from Washington and Idaho came in with expertise and heavy equipment. There was still no electricity, until Gil Berg managed to acquire two almost new diesel-powered generators from an Alaska fishing station for the bargain price of $5,000.

There were problems with the owners of the resort at Lucerne, who felt their business was threatened by the entry of any organization into Holden. Berg recalls that the Lucerne people tried in every way to discourage Holden development, even threatening legal action over the transporting of people to and from the Village. The resort people believed the Forest Service had given them an exclusive permit to transport visitors along the road from Lucerne to Holden. (By the early 1970s new resort operators and Holden had become friends and when the resort closed in 1976 its facilities were given to the Village; see Chapter Eight.)

Berg spearheaded the entire operation those first three years, directing not only the renovation work but also fundraising, general promotion, and the building of church relationships. Already in October 1960 he traveled to Minneapolis to meet with the national church youth directors. Along with a development council, Gil also organized promotional dinners in the Northwest and the Twin Cities, with as many as 1,200 attending.

"Gil was our natural leader from the start," Rieke remembers. "He had unbounded enthusiasm for the project."

Berg accepted no pay for any of his time in the service of Holden. Several years after he left the business manager post (1963) a grateful board put his name on Chalet One. Gil, who was born in 1899, continues to be active with his family in managing four Seattle area stitchery stores.

Another early key figure was Wilton Bergstrand. As youth director of the Augustana Lutheran Church, Wilt saw Holden immediately as a place for young adult ministry. His first visit came in December of 1960 when he and Berg studied the Village from the air in a light plane. The response of Bergie (as Bergstrand was called) was one of high and intense excitement. He became Holden's chief promoter in the church across the country.

So Berg and Bergie formed a team, the one managing the physical needs of Holden, the other looking for financial support and selling the idea of the Village as a facility of great potential for the church nationwide.

As early as January 1961 a call was issued inviting Bergstrand to become program director. After considering it for some time, he declined. Over the next two years he was asked twice more to assume staff leadership responsibilities at the Village, and both times he again said No. Bergstrand was torn between love for Holden and his desire to be involved in the shaping of youth ministry for the new Lutheran Church in America during the last years prior to its launching in 1963.

## Bergstrand and the Forerunners

But Wilt gave much to the Village nevertheless from 1961 until the spring of 1963. He contributed to the philosophy of what Holden could do for the church. He helped to assure Holden involvement by the youth program of the new LCA. Bergie and his wife Dolores led the month-long work crew in June and July of 1961, and returned for program leadership the summer of 1962 (Dolores for the entire summer).

That 1961 work camp was a remarkable experience for all who took part. Forty-one young adults (mostly college age, a few high-school seniors) paid their way to the Village. Food costs were covered by the Augustana and ALC youth offices. They cleaned all the buildings, repaired chimneys, cut hiking trails, rejuvenated lawns, entertained some 200 visitors, and (according to Bergstrand) "washed 9,779 windowpanes—after replacing at least 8,000 of them." They had daily Bible study led by Bergstrand and daily study of the natural environment led by Dr. Harold Leraas of Pacific Lutheran University. They also hosted a one-day visit by 71 delegates from the Augustana annual convention, which happened to be meeting in Seattle.

"We called ourselves the Forerunners," said Bergstrand, "after John the Baptist, the forerunner of Christ." And prepare the way they did! They were the ones who at last got the Village in shape for receiving guests.

Also in the summer of 1961 LBI hosted four successive weeks of Bible and nature study—one for 39 high-school youth, one for 36 adults, one for 50 in family groups, and one attended by several clergy families.

Much of the 1962 summer effort involved hosting visitors, many of whom were enroute to or from the Seattle World's Fair. A special three-day Holden experience was planned to help introduce the Village to Lutheran fairgoers from across the country. An informal, short-term program was offered, including Bible and environmental study, worship and an opportunity for hiking and fishing. Some 1500 came and Dolores Bergstrand was the hostess.

Wilt Bergstrand worked nearly full-time as a development person for the Village from January through March 1963. In addition, he made these contributions to Holden's start-up years as a Lutheran center:

● promoted the Village tirelessly, with speeches and by preparing early brochures, articles, and filmstrips;

● enlisted major financial support from individuals, the Augustana Luther League, and via offerings at various church gatherings;

● saw to it that the library and office equipment from the Augustana youth office were donated to Holden when that operation closed the end of 1962;

● recruited faculty persons Beanie Lundholm and Rudy Edmund from Augustana College, Rock Island, who became key Village figures;

● helped Holden acquire its organ through the gift of memorial funds following the death of his mother Esther in September 1962.

Bergstrand and Berg worked together well. Bergstrand thought it had something to do with the similarity in their Scandinavian names. "Berg means mountain," he noted, "and Bergstrand means mountain shore." Beyond that, "We understood and respected each other, and were united by the lordship of Christ and by the calm assurance that we were doing something creative for him!"

It has been observed by more than one person that "without Berg and Bergstrand Holden would not have gotten off the ground."

In 1963 Bergstrand took a call to be pastor of Holy Trinity Lutheran Church in Jamestown, New York, where he served until his retirement in 1984. He is now summer chaplain at Lutheran House in the nearby Chautauqua Institution; Dolores serves there as summer director of Lutheran House.

## Hinderlie Takes the Helm

By early 1963 the board knew that Bergstrand would not be available to direct the Holden program. It turned to Carroll Hinderlie, who had known of the Holden gift during 1960, his last year as youth director of the Evangelical Lutheran Church. After its merger into The ALC Carroll studied in Denmark on a Fulbright Scholarship, then served as a youth pastor at Westwood Lutheran Church in suburban Minneapolis and did some teaching at Luther Seminary in St. Paul. In March 1963, in his 50th year, Carroll accepted the board's call to be executive director at Holden. He began work full-time in late spring.

All who know Carroll would no doubt agree that they have never met anyone quite like him. He is a unique creation. And he, with his wife Mary, over the next 13-plus years would turn Holden Village into a unique creation.

When Carroll finished theological studies in 1940, he and Mary headed for missionary service in China. While still studying Chinese in the Philippines in 1941, they were herded with other civilian prisoners into a Japanese internment camp. Released at war's end in 1945, the Hinderlies returned to the States. Carroll served parish pastorates in Manitowoc, Wisconsin; Clear Lake, Iowa; and Watertown, South Dakota, for the next nine years. From 1954 through 1960 he was ELC youth director.

Hinderlie had mixed feelings about the Village when he was asked to become director. "I saw great potential there if it could become a retreat center for adults, such as we had seen in Europe. But I did not think it had much future with youth programing. I also wondered if our church was ready to support a creative center where lay people would be encouraged to think about their faith and their culture."

Dr. Fredrik Schiotz, ALC president at the time, urged Hinderlie to take the position. According to Carroll's recollection, "Schiotz thought it would probably fail, but he said I could stand a failure."

Seven or eight years later, when the ALC district bishops were at Holden and the close of the Schiotz presidency was being observed, Dr. Schiotz told them, "I can't help thinking it was God's will that Hinderlie be here, rather than teaching at a seminary, because here he was able to reach a far wider audience than future clergy alone."

A friend of the Hinderlies, Edna Hong, has written about Carroll and Mary and their unusual combination of attributes (see "Two Who Shaped Holden Village" in *Tapestry*, Augsburg, 1985). Edna observes that the Hinderlies are "too intellectual and scholarly to be evangelists" and "too evangelistic to be academics." Hong also opines that perhaps a place like Holden was just right for the gifts of people like Carroll and Mary Hinderlie. Many, including Fredrik Schiotz, agreed.

## "Holden Never Became Sterile"

That first Hinderlie summer at the Village was a mixture of plans laid by the national youth offices and elements introduced by Carroll. Joe Bash of the ALC youth staff had been designated earlier to serve as interim program director. He recalls "an abysmal failure with a projected pre-military-induction week" (nobody came), along with "an excellent week or two with family concerns and a young-adult stehekin that went well, led by Gordon Smedsrud"—also of the ALC national youth staff.

Some of the teaching faculty who have come to symbolize the Village at its best for decades of guests were brought by Hinderlie already in 1963: among them Fritz Norstad and Paul Heyne (along with Lundholm and Edmund, recruited by Bergstrand).

Carroll in his first report to the board (September 1963) said, "The remoteness of the Village must be made an asset. Distance, difficult access, a quiet boat trip—all play their part in preparation. Dr. Norstad, who has had pastors/wives clinics elsewhere, calls Holden 'a miracle,' saying 'Pastors and their families are more exposed here the first day than on the final day of our clinics.' "

Hinderlie then asked the board, "What is to be our image? A retreat center for training in 20th-century discipleship, a quiet place in the land where conversation takes place between persons exposed through the Spirit—this is what we have seen from this summer's operation."

And that is what Carroll and Mary stuck with unwaveringly through all their time at the Village. They had spent two summers in France and Norway helping build retreat centers and were solidly committed to the growth of retreat ministry this side of the Atlantic. But Carroll was skeptical about the readiness of the Lutheran community in North America for such an emphasis.

"We have the place before we have the mood or the movement to support the retreat concept in our Lutheran family," he wrote. The godparenting of that mood and movement within the Lutheran family on this continent may be the chief contribution made by Carroll and Mary. (The way Holden's retreat program evolved—summer only at first, and then year-around—is explored in the next two chapters.)

Gil Berg served with Carroll as business manager for half a year. They had differences in both style and vision. Having worked also with Wilt Bergstrand, Berg observes that "if Bergstrand had accepted the call to be director Holden would have developed in quite another way. He and Hinderlie are as different as night and day." Berg then goes on to say, "I give Carroll credit for bringing such interesting people up there. You didn't want to go to bed at night because you were in such fascinating arguments. That was Carroll's great strength— he never let Holden become sterile!"

## "Free in the Gospel"

Jean Swihart, who worked with drama and children's programs and beautification of the grounds and many other aspects of Village life from 1963 until her death in the fall of 1986, said, "Carroll put a stamp on Holden that I hope will always be there. He let us be ourselves and let us be free in the Gospel."

Jean had been recruited by Doris Edmund to help set up a Village program for children. She also worked to get craft programs started in the early years. Jean enjoyed telling of the young engineer from Boeing named Werner Janssen who was managing the food service in the summer of 1963.

"One day Carroll said he needed someone to serve as business manager in place of Gil Berg. I casually mentioned Werner as a possibility. That evening Carroll informed the Village that Werner would be the new Holden business manager, which was great. Except that Carroll had not yet gotten Werner's assent. That incident says something about Carroll's unique style."

Werner did agree to serve, and he stayed from November 1963 through September 1984 (the last year on a consulting basis). His service through all of the Hinderlie, Norstad, and Schramm administrations makes Werner easily the longest-tenured Holden Village staff person.

If it's true that "Berg and Bergie got Holden off the ground," it's equally true that the Hinderlies set its flight path and kept it soaring, and that Werner Janssen, the Boeing engineer, made sure it always stayed in fine flying condition.

# 4 The Summer Program

*Carroll and Mary Hinderlie built a Village that is one of
the wonders of the life of the church in our time.*
*—Fritz Norstad, Village director 1977-78*

The summer program, that which happens at Holden Village
from June through September, is the only face of Holden known
to about 80% of the 5,500 annual Villagers. Indeed, until the
early 1970s it was the only Holden Village there was. Winter
programing did not begin until 1972-73.

That first summer of receiving guests, 1961, the program
was limited. Four weeks from mid-July to mid-August, featuring study of the Bible and study of the creation, were offered
by Lutheran Bible Institute of Seattle. Pastor Erman Lunder
of the LBI faculty, who directed those weeks, remembers that
time as "very therapeutic, because people who were working
hard with their hands to renovate the Village also took time
for Bible study and prayer." Lunder recalls that a general open
house for individuals and groups, who came both to work and
to have a look at the Village, continued into October of 1961.
Though the program was at best a limited one, some 500 people
found their way to the Village during 1961, nearly all during
the summer and early fall.

By the summer of 1962 there had been time for a bit more
program planning. A program committee included three national youth leaders (Pastors Joe Bash, Wilt Bergstrand, Cal
Storley) and Pastor Bob Rismiller of the LBI faculty. Management of each program segment was the responsibility of a
designated person.

## Stehekin—the Way Through

Among the 1962 offerings was a young-adult program (August 6-17) called "stehekin," an Indian word meaning "the way through" (it is also the name of the small town at the north end of Lake Chelan). Young-adult stehekins were a regular summer element for the next several years. One participant in Holden's first stehekin was Carol Nolte, now a Lutheran pastor in Los Angeles and a member of Holden's board. Carol recalls:

> I saw an ad in the *Lutheran Companion* (magazine of the Augustana Church) and decided to stop in on my way to the Seattle World's Fair. C. Umhau Wolff, a pastor from Toledo, Ohio, was the leader, and Elmer Witt of the Walther League was our chaplain. I went on to the fair in Seattle but it was so boring that I quickly came back to Holden and worked for several weeks. I decided to return in 1963 and worked almost the entire summer, primarily on sorting through materials from the mine office with Rudy Edmund. I've been at the Village for at least a little while almost every summer since.

Participation increased significantly for the summer of 1962, compared to 1961. Total for the year was 1,600, nearly all during June through August. In program terms the Village was still finding its way. It was becoming clear that a permanent, full-time person who could direct program development was needed.

At the first General Convention of the new American Lutheran Church that October, delegates were told by the youth board that Holden would have a special focus on older youth and young adults and on training those who work professionally with youth. The report also indicated that Holden's first full program would be offered the summer of 1963.

One of the features planned for 1963, the pre-induction conference for young people entering military service, was endorsed by the 1962 ALC convention. Its resolution encouraged congregations to prepare service-bound youth "to become witnessing Christians" and to use "the pre-induction camp at Holden Village" as a vehicle. Unfortunately, the event was never held because of insufficient registration.

One 1963 use of the Village by military personnel did occur, however. A spiritual-life retreat for Air Force personnel was scheduled for a week in August. It was basically organized by Air Force chaplains, who brought their own program with them. It remained an annual summer occurrence through 1965. In some ways the military style did not fit Holden's informality and egalitarian approach to community. Carol Nolte remembers that there were arguments over whether the Air Force personnel could be paired randomly for roommate purposes (Holden's way) or whether they had to be paired according to rank (the Air Force preference).

The entry of such outside groups was more than welcome in the early years, when the Village needed every bit of help to pay the bills. Also, the initial agreement with the U.S. Forest Service specified that the Village should be available to outside groups when the facilities were not filled by Holden's own program (and the understanding continues that anyone from the general public may come to Holden as a guest). It was not until the early 1970s that Holden was filled all summer by its own constituency. Another outside user was Camp Farthest Out. A theologically conservative group emphasizing care of creation and physical wellness, CFO was not really a misfit at the Village. People remember that among its leaders one summer was the late Jean Carter Stapleton, evangelist who later became well known as President Jimmy Carter's sister.

## Who's in Charge Here?

That summer of 1963 "first full program" had been planned during the preceding months by representatives of the national youth boards and Seattle LBI. The ALC's Joe Bash served as on-site program director from mid-June until mid-August.

But Carroll Hinderlie, who had assumed the Village directorship at the start of the summer, also brought some of his own choices as 1963 summer faculty. Among them were Richard Luecke, a Missouri Synod theologian from Chicago: Rudy Edmund, geology professor from Augustana College, Rock Island, Illinois; and Fritz Norstad, theology professor from Luther Seminary in St. Paul. Norstad says he "became hooked on the Village from that first summer." Participation for the year 1963 was nearly 2,500, virtually all of it summer attenders. It remained at approximately that level through 1968.

The summer of 1963 was one of the coldest and wettest on record in the Railroad Creek Valley. Participants recall that it was especially unpleasant because there was no heat in many of the buildings, and only fireplace heat in the livingrooms of chalets. That summer also launched the tradition of Christmas in July, still celebrated annually on the 25th of the month. "We began it," says Carroll Hinderlie, "because we felt Christmas should be celebrated at Holden, but in those days there was no community at the Village on the 25th of December."

The 1964 summer program was developed jointly by the youth staffs and Hinderlie. It covered 11 weeks, from mid-June to late August. Faculty names included Armin Grams, Norman Habel, Beanie Lundholm, Rudy Edmund, Arnold Flaten, Howard Hong, Fritz Norstad, George Aus, George Forell, plus national youth leaders Elmer Witt (LCMS), Carl Manfred (LCA), Joe Bash (ALC), and Mert Strommen (Lutheran Youth Research). Camp Farthest Out and the Air Force retreat were back for a week each.

Already in 1963, and even more the next year, it became obvious that program leadership would need to be lodged either with the youth departments or with the Village director; it could not be done well with two heads. Partly, it was the classic issue of role confusion between members of an organization's board and its chief staff person. But there were larger questions: what program focus should the Village develop and who should be its primary constituency? The national youth boards continued to have an investment in their initial dream: that the Village be chiefly a place for young adults and for training of leaders for youth ministry in general. But Carroll Hinderlie's vision, despite his background in denominational youth ministry, was that Holden needed to be a center for all ages, with an emphasis on lay adults, yet with space for children and youth in family groups.

The debate went on within the board for a couple of years. At the same time the board was becoming more directly the creature of the youth departments. The board initially created in December 1960 had included fairly strong representation from national youth boards. But a 1963 restructuring gave 15 voting seats to the national church bodies (five each to ALC, LCA, and LCMS), and the youth boards had the responsibility for appointing these people. One of the ALC spots was given to Erman Lunder of the LBI faculty, who continued on the board through 1978 and was its secretary the entire time. There were also advisory seats for the LBI president, for the Lutheran colleges and seminaries, and for Lutheran Youth Research (a Minneapolis-based inter-Lutheran entity).

## Rieke Keeps Heads Cool

The debate over program focus was complicated by financial reality. It was clear to everyone that, as Luvern Rieke recalls, "In those early years the Village simply would not have survived without the financial contributions from the youth boards." The Village also received modest grants during the 1960s from the ALC men's organization and its social service division.

The strong leadership of board chairman Rieke helped ease the tensions surrounding the program orientation debate. Joe Bash remembers, "Vern heard all sides with respect and kept heads cool when eruptions seemed likely. As our chair he brought the Village a stature one could not miss."

Within a couple of years most of the youth ministry people on the board had come to agree with Hinderlie about the broader approach the Village needed to take.

"The family orientation for Holden was also promoted by young adults themselves," says Vern Rieke. "Whether serving as volunteer staff or participating in the stehekin program, the young adults argued strongly for a transgenerational Village."

By the summer of 1965, only the young-adult stehekin was still directed by the youth departments. The board at its October 1965 meeting voted that the director should assume responsibility for all of the Village program, including stehekin, but to plan program "in consultation with the youth offices of the three supporting churches." The board stressed also that the youth units should continue their modest subsidies to the Village. Finally, the board voted that Holden should limit high-school groups to seniors, but that "youth of all ages are welcome with their families."

The amount of subsidy from the three national youth offices totaled approximately $20,000 annually from 1963 through 1966. During those four years the Village budget grew from $41,000 to $143,000. With 1968 the grant from the Lutheran Church in America ended and the financial support from The American Lutheran Church and the Lutheran Church—Missouri Synod were cut in half. By 1970 all denominational youth department grants had ceased. A 1971 revision of the Village bylaws removed reference to association with national church youth ministries, but retained designation of certain board members as "representing the national church bodies," a pattern continued to the present.

One other indication of the shift in program focus from the beginning to the end of the 1960s: in its report to each biennial convention from 1962 through 1970 the ALC youth office included discussion of Holden Village; after 1970 the Village is not mentioned in those convention reports.

## Summer Program Themes

The practice of giving no cash payment and no travel expenses to teaching staff—only free room and board for their immediate family—began early in the Hinderlie administration. Faculty recruitment has never been a problem. (Current director Elmer Witt reports that the Village receives some 125 unsolicited offers from would-be teachers annually.) Hinderlie had no trouble attracting big-name theologians and church leaders to the Village for two or three summer weeks; indeed, some stayed up to a couple of months. Among the Hinderlie recruits were the Quaker scholar Roland Bainton, Roman Catholic theologian Rosemary Ruether, and Lutheran historian Martin Marty.

Other internationally known figures appearing at Holden over the years have included Conrad Bergendoff, John DeGruchy, John Howard Yoder, Leo Bustad, Ron Sider, and John Taylor.

The Lutheran Institute for Theological Education has brought to Holden such leaders as Robert McAfee Brown, Zephaniah Kameeta, Walter Wangerin, and Helmut Thielicke. (Thielicke speaks of "amazing Holden" in his autobiography.)

Both Carroll and Mary Hinderlie themselves took active roles in the teaching from the first—leading Bible studies, stimulating theological discussion, and creating excitement around great literature. Edna Hong concludes that, thanks to the Hinderlie style, "Holden Village has created more lay theologians than any other lay institute in the Lutheran church" of North America.

Carol Nolte remembers that the Hinderlies "stressed literature a lot. C. S. Lewis, Charles Williams, and Dorothy Sayers were especially important to them. They had books everywhere in their chalet, even in the kitchen cupboards."

Jean Swihart, a summer regular virtually every year between 1963 and 1986, said she "didn't know women could be theologians until I discovered Holden. It was also the place where my 12-year-old daughter first experienced women writing books and doing things other than being housewives and mothers."

Many, many women have served as teachers at Holden. Women have also been prominent among those serving as Village pastors: Nancy Winder 1976-78, Susan Kyllo 1985-86, and Barbara Rossing 1986 to the present.

Beginning with 1965, Carroll Hinderlie proposed annual summer program themes to the board, starting a tradition that has continued to the present. "Training for 20th-Century Discipleship" was the 1965 theme. Among those used in later years have been:

    1967—"Christ Is Risen: the Whole Earth Is His"
    1968—"Think and Thank (Gratitude in a Complaining World)"
    1970—"For Freedom Christ Has Set Us Free"
    1972—"Amazing Grace"
    1976—"Let Freedom Ring That Love May Abound"
    1980—"Faith To Go Out with Good Courage"
    1981—"Sing the Lord's Song"
    1985—"In the Shadow of God's Wings"
    1986—"Gentle Justice"
    1987—"Christ Is the Memory of Our Future"

The Hinderlies also carved out a central role for humor in all aspects of Village life. What came to be known as "holy hilarity" marked everything from garbage pickup to creative liturgies for the most mundane occasions to witty Village song lyrics. The first song, "A Place Apart," was created by Doris Edmund and Beanie Lundholm in the summer of 1963. Later, Doris teamed with Philip Brunelle, an inventive Twin Cities musician, to write many of the whimsical song lyrics that are still being sung at Holden.

"I always believed we needed to laugh at the Village," says Carroll, "so it could never become an idolatry. We didn't want Holden to be taken too seriously. It had to remain fragile so the Holy Spirit could move it out once it was no longer useful to God's Kingdom."

## Summer Participation Peaks by Mid-70s

The basic summer schedule known today had evolved already by the mid-1960s: Bible study after breakfast, a variety of presentations and discussions the rest of the forenoon; afternoon basically open for individual pursuits such as craft work or short hikes, perhaps a book discussion; evenings given to full community gathering for Vespers plus a program session or two. From the beginning it was understood that any guest's daily pattern was to be unstructured and informal, with full freedom to take part in as much or as little as one wished. The only daily expectation for everyone was attendance at Vespers.

Also from the earliest days, guests were permitted to come and go on any day of the week, though Saturday and Sunday have been most popular for arriving and departing. A typical guest visit has always been seven days. That continues to be the length of stay chosen by a majority of the summer Villagers. In 1986, 14% stayed one to three days, 28% four to six, 53% seven, and only 5% more than seven.

Program sessions in the early years met in the schoolhouse (now known as Narnia) or outdoors, with full community gatherings in the Village Center. After the remodeling of a lodge to create the present Koinonia space (finished in 1966), that became the usual location of group meetings, along with the Village Center. Small groups, from the first, have also met in chalet livingrooms and porches.

The Holden summer program has always included outdoor recreation—especially hiking and fishing—along with intellectual and spiritual stimulation. Organized sports never took hold at the Village, except for a tradition, born in the Hinderlie years, of volleyball following the evening meal.

Village attendance grew annually during the first decade. From a June/July/August daily population average (guests and staff, including children) of 172 in 1964, it climbed to 280 by 1969 and reached 343 in 1974. Attaining a summer-long average of around 350 meant there were as many as 425 or more in the Village on many mid-summer days. Indeed, in the first half of the 1970s Holden was often so full that staff had to eat outdoors and to let guests sleep in their beds. In recent years the Village has been considered full at 400. Average daily summer population was in the 350s in 1981 and 1982, again in 1986, but it was spread more evenly throughout the entire three months than had been true in the early 1970s. Since the latter 1970s, September has also been near capacity, though of course with few school-age children.

## The Great Transition

By the mid-1970s it was clear that, whatever Holden Village had become under Lutheran auspices, it was surely a success, whether one used program or financial measures. It had developed a large and loyal constituency. The Hinderlie vision and leadership had accomplished that, without any doubt.

"Carroll came to us with tremendous enthusiasm and energy, and a well-developed set of ideas for the Village," Luvern Rieke recalls. "He had great strength as a communicator of the Gospel. He was also able to stimulate financial support from private sources. It is impossible to imagine the Village as we know it today without the gifts and the service of Carroll Hinderlie."

Carroll had expected to spend his remaining years of ministry as director of Holden, which would have kept him at the helm until 1981 or 1982. But administrative problems and personnel tensions at the Village became matters of serious concern in the latter part of 1976. Early in 1977 the board decided it was time to make a leadership change. Carroll was given a three-year contract, through the end of 1979, as Holden's theologian-at-large. He would do speaking and fund-raising for Holden outside the Village. Fritz Norstad, a close and long-time associate of Carroll, agreed to leave, a year earlier than planned, his work directing the human ecology program at Lutheran General Hospital in Chicago, in order to become Holden's interim director.

The leave-taking was painful for Carroll and Mary. In a farewell letter to the Holden trustees, Carroll spoke of the hurt. But he also mentioned the affirmation he felt when told that ALC President David Preus had recently in a sermon cited Hinderlie's Holden leadership to illustrate how God uses people in unexpected ways. Preus also quoted Hinderlie as referring to himself as "God's joke," and that pleased Carroll.

Not only had Carroll been director for nearly 14 years, in terms of program leadership he was the only director the Village had ever had. It is not possible to overstate the towering influence he and Mary had in shaping the Village those 14 years. Nor was it limited to the summer program, as later chapters will indicate. Their contribution is the one that still flavors Holden most pungently, more than a decade later.

So it is not surprising that, as the 1977 changes occurred, just one question was in the mind of everyone who cared about

Holden: "Could the Village survive without the Hinderlie leadership?"

Fritz Norstad had been a regular Village teacher since 1963. He was also a long-time dear friend of the Hinderlies (he and Carroll were St. Olaf College freshmen together) and he had championed Carroll's candidacy for director 14 years before. The Hinderlies, though not happy about leaving Holden, were completely happy with the selection of Norstad as interim director.

Nevertheless, Norstad says he was viewed by many among the friends of the Village with suspicion and "as an interloper" when he assumed the task. Norstad says he felt the board acted responsibly in making a change in leadership, that it was time for a change. "As happens with most new enterprises, the Village had become something like an inverted triangle, resting on the point which was its prime shaper, Carroll Hinderlie. There is intense anxiety when that point is removed. In the view of many, the Village itself was threatened, and might not survive. In time, the triangle was turned to rest on a broader base. The board took more leadership. More people and different kinds of people began coming as staff and as guests."

Norstad is quick to add, "I also know to this day that Carroll and Mary built a Village that is one of the wonders of the life of the church in our time."

## "Right Person, Right Time"

Ellen Gamrath of Mercer Island, Washington, who had been a board member since 1972 (and with her family an active Village participant since 1963) succeeded Rieke as board chair in 1978. Ellen notes that "God has always provided the right person for Holden at the right time. This was true when Carroll became director, with his vision of a lay theological retreat center and his willingness to beg for money to make that dream

**THE GIFT.** In formal transfer of Holden to Lutheran Bible Institute of Seattle, October 1960, unidentified attorney for Howe Sound Company (left), presents papers to President E. V. Stime of Seattle LBI (right). At center is Gil Berg, Holden manager for the Lutherans (photo by Johnson Studio, Seattle). BELOW. Group of work campers prepares to leave Village in scene from summer of 1962; note still-standing Chalet Two (photo by Frederick H. Gonnerman).

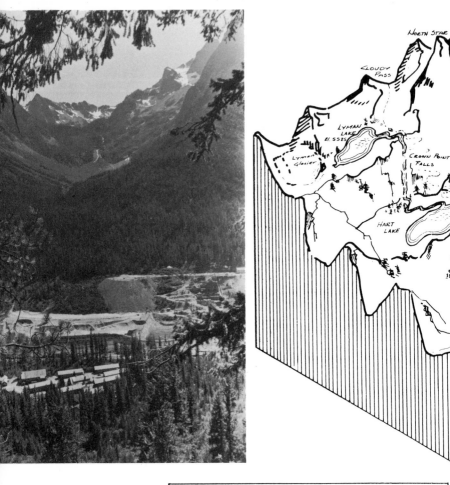

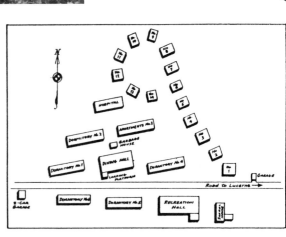

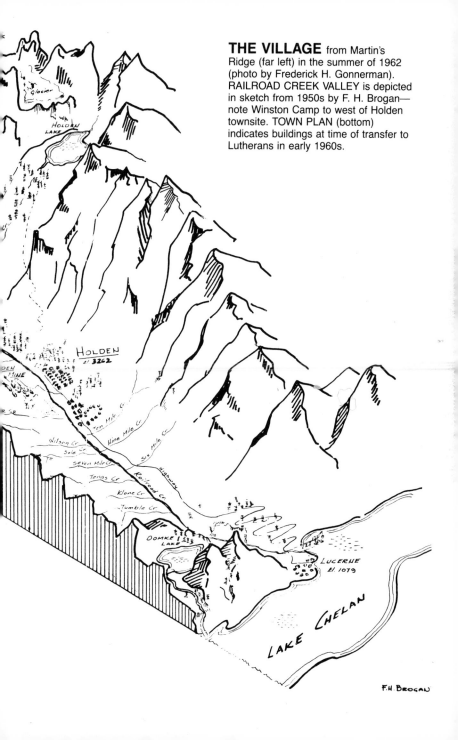

**THE VILLAGE** from Martin's Ridge (far left) in the summer of 1962 (photo by Frederick H. Gonnerman). RAILROAD CREEK VALLEY is depicted in sketch from 1950s by F. H. Brogan— note Winston Camp to west of Holden townsite. TOWN PLAN (bottom) indicates buildings at time of transfer to Lutherans in early 1960s.

Glacier

HOLDEN LAKE

HOLDEN
el. 3262

DEN MINE

R CR

Wilson Cr
Sole Cr
Seven Mile Cr
Tenns Cr
Klone Cr
Tumble Cr

Ten Mile Cr
Nine Mile Cr
Six Mile Cr
Highway
Railroad Cr

OOMKE LAKE

LUCERNE
el. 1079

LAKE CHELAN

F.H. BROGAN

**VOLUNTEER** work campers in summers of 1961 and 1962 tackled many tasks to ready Village for guests. In these 1962 scenes, trail clearing and window cleaning have the focus (photos by Frederick H. Gonnerman).

a reality. It was sheer gift when Fritz Norstad was available and willing to come ahead of his planned retirement, and again true in the sequence of events that brought John Schramm to the Village and to the present with the coming of Elmer Witt."

Norstad believes that Holden has shown "it has a life of its own and a vitality that could carry it through the grief and anger of the Hinderlie separation. It had its gospel. It took its first change in directors in stride. Credit for that goes both to the Hinderlies and to the board of directors."

Norstad was not able to take over direction of the Village until late spring of 1977. Between January and his arrival the board had asked a seminary intern, Ron Vignec, to serve as Village program coordinator, while Werner Janssen was to be responsible for Village operations.

## Miners' Reunion in 1977

One highlight of Norstad's year came the summer of 1977 with a reunion for people who had lived at Holden during its mining years. Werner Janssen had conceived the celebration to recognize the 20th anniversary of the mine's closing. The event was organized in consultation with Nigel Adams (the mine historian—see Chapter Two) and other former residents who lived nearby. Some 230 happy people came on a chartered boat for the day, August 13, spending about six hours in the Village. The plaque they presented that day (Chapter Two) is now in the Portal, Holden's museum, along with messages of gratitude and photographs from the reunion.

A board search committee, chaired by Pastor Bill Dierks, then serving an LCMS parish at Mercer Island, Washington, worked through all of 1977 on the quest for a new permanent director. By the end of the year the board had issued a call to Pastor John Schramm, who accepted and agreed to begin a six-year term on April 1, 1978.

John and Mary Schramm at the time were living on a farm in West Virginia. Both were nationally known in church circles as speakers and writers on social justice and peace themes. John was working in a part-time peace education assignment for an ALC national board. Earlier he had served two pastorates in the Washington, D.C., area and had directed the Lutheran social service agency in the nation's capitol.

"That first summer was difficult," John says. "Carroll and I are very different, so the comparisons that inevitably came were hard. No matter who followed a strong personality like Carroll, it would have to be demonstrated that the Village could live and thrive under different leadership. I knew that was part of the challenge when I took the job. But the Village has a life and is a place of renewal entirely apart from who happens to be its director."

## The Schramm Emphases

In terms of summer program emphasis, the Schramm years are probably remembered most for their central focus on issues of social justice. The chief theological theme those six years was the theology of the cross with its stress on God's entering into the suffering of humanity and its renunciation of theological triumphalism. A related theme, the theology of enough, was a prominent program element. Both personal/family consumption patterns and the life-style of the Village as community were rigorously examined in terms of sufficiency and simplicity. (For more on Holden's consumption styles, see Chapter Seven.)

Other new summer program features of the Schramm years included introduction of an annual week for hearing-impaired people. And one summer a group of retarded adults was brought from a sheltered workshop in Wenatchee. An effort was undertaken to make the Village as physically accessible as is possible in mountain terrain. One can now come to Holden in a wheelchair and get around fairly well.

John also brought in program directors for each summer (Mary Hinderlie had served in that role during the previous period). Walter Boumann, Charlie Mays, and Larry Rasmussen shared that responsibility from 1978 through 1983. They assembled the summer teaching staff and coordinated the entire adult learning program. John believed a maximum number of people ought to be able to have the experience of teaching at Holden. He thus encouraged the use of new people and larger numbers of people, with the inevitable result that there were shorter stays by some long-time regulars from the Hinderlie years. The practice of paying teachers only with room and board for themselves and their family members was continued. And the practice of expecting teachers and their spouses to take turns on dish teams became firmly established. It was a revival of the mode of the earliest years, when not only teachers but guests as well put in time with Village work crews.

Both Mary and John Schramm taught regularly. John led discussions on the theology of the cross, nonviolence, social action and the contemplative life, and the theology of enough, in addition to preaching regularly. Mary offered sessions on the evoking of one's gifts and the life-style of peacemaking, led book discussions, and handled most of the orientation for each day's new arrivals. Mary also managed the Village bookstore all six years, developing it into an outstanding resource.

"We had only three givens at the Village," John recalls. "One, Vespers is for everyone every night. Two, no use of drugs. Three, the proclamation that Jesus is Lord was not up for vote, though we tried to make welcome those who had another affirmation. I felt all three were quite well accepted while we were at Holden."

The Schramms decided to leave Holden after six years in order to undertake some new forms of ministry. They left in the spring of 1984 and located in Minneapolis, where both became instrumental in the formation of the Community of St. Martin, an ecumenical community focusing on peace and justice. In December 1984 Mary opened a bookstore/restaurant named St. Martin's Table, which she continues to manage. John took on part-time assignments with the mission discovery program of the ALC and on the pastoral staff of Trinity Lutheran Congregation in Minneapolis. Both Mary and John continue in nationwide demand as speakers and writers.

## Witt Is Next

As the next director of Holden the board chose Elmer Witt, a pastor of the Association of Evangelical Lutheran Churches, who began a six-year term on April 1, 1984. Elmer's association with Holden dated from its Lutheran beginnings. He had been executive director of the Walther League, a youth organization affiliated with the Lutheran Church—Missouri Synod, at the time the Village was given to the church. He was an early supporter of LCMS participation, became a member of the board as early as 1962, and secured Walther League financial support throughout the 1960s. Elmer had spent the 1972-84 period in Lutheran campus ministry, but had served frequently on the Holden summer teaching staff between 1967 and 1983.

After accepting the call and before starting work as director, Elmer suffered the death of his wife Virginia. It meant that he was deep in the grief process as he began his new ministry. "The Holden community was a healing place for me to be at that time," Elmer recalls. "I am grateful for the love and care of many people in those months of my beginning at the Village."

Witt came to Holden "determined to retain the essence of what the Village had been, which is primarily the renewal and growth of adults. But I have also wanted us to do a better job of respecting the right of children and youth to have their own identifiable activities."

He has also sought to bring greater variety and more inclusivity to the summer teaching staff: "more non-ordained, non-Lutherans, and non-Americans, more women, and more persons of color."

Theologically, Elmer sees the doctrine of creation as central for Holden. "I want us to be able to understand the First Article of the Creed as grace, not just as law."

Elmer has also utilized summer program coordinators, with Norm Folkerts (1984), Herman Diers (1985), Ingrid Christiansen and Jody Kretzmann (1986), and Jack and Sarah Nelson-Pallmeyer (1987) in that function.

## Three Directors, Three Styles

And so Holden Village continues, now with its third permanent director in 25 years. Three Gospel-captured men, but each quite different from the other two. Surely with each director the Village has taken on much of his unique personality. And yet the Village has shown that it is more than its director. It has, as Fritz Norstad said, "a life of its own." It is resilient—able to absorb and incorporate the distinctive gifts brought by each leader, yet suffering little damage from the inevitable failings of each.

● ● ●

Holden's summer program is the only Holden most Villagers ever see. It also provides the support base for the rest of the year: without the paying summer guests, including the voluntary contributions they make as donors to the Village, the winter program could not exist. Yet, there is always a bit of tension for Holden between being a year-around community and being an operation for guests who come in the summer months. Are the summer Villagers "outsiders"? To ask it another way, "Whose Village is it, anyway?"

Looking at the winter Holden, the October-through-May Holden, will lead us into such questions.

# 5 The Rest of the Year

*The fact that the boat doesn't go daily makes for a peace,
a relaxation, a contemplative mood. The pace is so different. And an intimacy develops which creates a strain
for many who are present the whole winter. You can't get
away from each other.*
*—Ellen Gamrath, Holden board chair 1978-86 and fre-
quent winter Villager*

Holden Village is a strikingly different place in the winter,
the months from October through May. "Winter" doesn't mean
it's bitter cold for eight months, though the first big snows
usually come in early November and the last can be as late as
early June. "Winter" at Holden is simply the designation for
"the rest of the year," the time other than the summer season
of June through September.

Holden was not initially seen by its Lutheran custodians as
a year-around operation. Since 1961-62, somebody has lived
there every winter to watch the property. But it wasn't until
Holden's second decade that winter programing began.

## Living with Winter Weather

The most basic reality in the winter Village is weather. It is
not unpleasant—never the sub-zero temperatures for days on
end known in the Upper Midwest, and hardly ever any significant winds. Winter weather at Holden means SNOW. From
the time of the first big snowfall until late in the spring, snow
dominates. A typical winter sees more than 200" of it. And
the snow can accumulate to a depth of 10 or 12 feet, even

more near the buildings as it slides off the roofs in massive piles.

All that snow means mobility to and from Lucerne on Lake Chelan is changed dramatically. It means a shift to vehicles with treads that can move across the surface of the snow. It means no sunlight through first-floor windows much of the season and digging snow stairways down into Village buildings. It means being wary of avalanches of snow sliding off the roofs with no warning. It also means excellent cross-country skiing and snowshoeing.

Another difference in the winter is the schedule maintained by the Lake Chelan Boat Company. Lake Chelan never freezes—its depth and mild temperatures prevent it. But traffic is sharply reduced on the lake from October through April. So for most of that period the boat makes only three roundtrips a week—on Mondays, Wednesdays, and Fridays. Compared with summer, that creates an obvious change in the daily Village rhythm. On four days each week there are no arrivals and no departures. And that makes the three boat days also seem unusual. It all creates quite a different pace. Ellen Gamrath believes it "makes for a peace, a relaxation, a contemplative mood."

The combination of heavy snows and the non-daily boat schedule underscores the reality, more easily forgotten in the summer, that Holden truly is a remote place, always captive to its environment. It produces an awareness of our vulnerability to the natural order, one that is largely obscured for today's urban dwellers.

The snow, the change in pace, and the relatively small winter population combine to fashion a much different community feeling. Before discussing that difference in detail, let us explore how the winter Village came to be.

## Group Home for Boys

Holden's winter program evolved slowly. No one lived in the Village the winter of 1960-61, and only one or two persons were there through each of the next five winters. With the winter of 1966-67 it was decided to experiment with keeping the Village open year-around, allowing guests to come if they wished.

"Three of us stayed that entire winter," says Werner Janssen, then the Village business manager. They were the newlywed Janssens (Judy Meek and Werner had married the previous September) and Terry Sateren, a sculptor who created Holden's dancing servant sculpture. "Even though we offered no program, we did maintain the Village worship life throughout that winter," Werner recalls. "About 20 people came as paying guests, all staying in Chalet One."

Werner recalls that 1966 began the tradition of having home-baked Christmas cookies brought by Loretta and Howard Gylling. Howard, an auditor from Seattle, served on the Village board for many years and continues to be its auditor.

The Janssens and a few others stayed through the winter of 1967-68 as well, and opened Chalet Two along with Chalet One for guest accommodations. For the winter of 1968-69 about 30 people stayed throughout. Christmas of 1968 was the first one with a significant number of guests present.

On a quiet afternoon in January of 1969 the Village learned a lesson about the particular danger of wintertime fire, when Chalet Two burned. The fire alarm could not be readily heard because it was covered by snow and few were around to hear it in any case. After a 20-minute struggle to get hoses in operation it was found that the closest hydrant was frozen. Hoses were eventually employed to dampen neighboring Chalets One and Three, and since there was no wind and the walls fell inward, other buildings were spared.

Plans to rebuild Chalet Two were made immediately, and there was strong hope it could be completed by 1971 as part of a 10th anniversary project. But the hole remains. So does the foundation, and the board keeps alive the plan to rebuild, if funds can be found. Only one other building has been lost to fire since the Lutherans took over: a garage near the mine site burned in October of 1977. It was replaced by the present A-frame building, quickly, in a three-week rush job that just beat the first heavy snowfall.

The first major element of winter program came in 1970-71. The board in 1969 had responded positively to a request from the Washington Division of Public Assistance that Holden become a group home for boys. The program began the following summer with six teenage boys. The group home was part of the Village year-around from that point until 1973, when it became a nine-month (school year) program.

While the effort consumed much staff energy, it had positive results for both the boys and the Village community. Most of the boys said their time at Holden was the first experience with a caring, loving family they'd ever had. A number of them asked to be baptized while at Holden. And the community provided a safe place for them to work on their problems. Many people were saddened when the program ended in 1979 because of a new state regulation requiring that group homes have the services of a counseling psychologist available.

## Lifestyle Enrichment Begins

During the 1971-72 period, discussion of a winter-long program for young adults became serious. Carroll Hinderlie recalls, "It was not my idea. Werner Janssen and John Graber had the vision for it." Graber was a St. Olaf College graduate with a master of fine arts from the University of Iowa. He offered a proposal for a program called Lifestyle Enrichment.

The board accepted it, hired John to direct it, and authorized its beginning with the 1972-73 school year.

Six persons were enrolled the first year: most were recent high-school graduates; the oldest had finished junior year of college. For the second year the program expanded to 12 students.

Lifestyle Enrichment continued as a nine-month program each winter through the 1977-78 season. In some years as many as 20 persons were enrolled. Then evolved a winter program of two sessions; currently, each runs for 10 weeks, from early October through mid-December and from early February through mid-April. The participants, typically 10 to 12 per term, become part of the Village community in all respects. Their study around a theological theme is guided by a Holden staff person, assisted by others who happen to be in the Village. Each participant has a part-time work assignment, and there is time for involvement in arts, crafts, and outdoor recreation. Total cost for a 10-week session was $650 in 1986-87. Minimum age is 18.

January for many years has been utilized by a Lutheran college for an interim course, usually focusing on some combination of theological and environmental studies. St. Olaf College of Northfield, Minnesota, and Pacific Lutheran University of Tacoma, Washington, have come in alternating years, and California Lutheran has also sponsored interim groups. The schools bring their own faculty with the students but also use Village resource persons.

As the winter community became an established reality, the Village also began to be used as a location for sabbaticals, mostly by pastors but occasionally by academics and others as well.

As families began living at the Village throughout the year, it became obvious that some provision for the education of children would need to be made. When the group home began in 1970, the Village provided a volunteer teacher who worked in consultation with the Chelan school district. Beginning with 1972-73, the Chelan district placed two paid teachers in the Village—one elementary, one secondary—an arrangement still in place. Teachers are picked and paid by the Chelan district, but it has been careful to choose people who are compatible with the spirit of the Village. School enrollment has varied from as few as 5 to as many as 22. The teachers regularly bring parents and other Villagers into the classroom, and there is a sense of total community involvement in education that is lacking in most public schools today.

The Hinderlies did not live at the Village year-around. They maintained a home in Minneapolis and, later, in Seattle. Carroll gave major attention to promoting Holden throughout the country and to Village fund-raising during the winter months. The Norstads did winter at the Village during Fritz's tenure as director, as have John and Mary Schramm and Elmer Witt.

Short-term retreats have been scheduled increasingly during recent winters. Some run Monday through Friday, some Friday to Sunday. Church councils and other congregational groups with their own agendas are also welcomed for retreats at Holden and the staff offers assistance with program planning for such groups. Further, individuals, couples, and families are encouraged to schedule retreat time at the Village during winter months.

## A Typical Winter Calendar

In even-numbered years, summer's end and transition to winter season at Holden is marked by a late-September week for clergy couples sponsored by the Lutheran Institute for Theological Education, a continuing education program affiliated with Pacific Lutheran University. With that week the pool hall and bowling alley also close for the season.

The rhythm of the next several months will take something like the following form:

- Early October—first term of winter study/work program begins.

- On an October weekend there may be a Holden-style homecoming, with touch football game, parade, and other attractions. In 1986 the community of Stehekin at the north end of Lake Chelan was invited and about 25 people came for the 24-hour celebration.

- November 11—St. Martin of Tours Day and U.S. Veterans Day—is observed with a world peace emphasis.

- Sometime before the middle of November the first heavy snowfall can be expected.

- Advent features weekend retreats and "Advent angels"—members of the community secretly adopt another community person for special care and acts of grace.

- During the week before and the week following Christmas Day, 50 or 60 guests may come to the Village. Throughout the two weeks, special Bible study, worship, and group discussions are scheduled. There are tree-cutting excursions and an elaborate Christmas pageant.

- On New Year's Day the Village may schedule a Snow Bowl football game.

- The college interim group arrives early in January and stays for most of the month.

- Martin Luther King Day in January is observed with a half-day holiday from work and with special worship.

- Second session of winter study/work program begins early in February.

- Some time around the middle of February comes SOB Day. That's "Sun Over Buckskin" Day, the first time since the previous fall that the morning sun, viewed from Village mainstreet, passes entirely above the peak of Buckskin Mountain. To assure themselves spring is near at hand, Vil!agers have a cookout on the loading dock.

● Good Friday to Easter weekend is a popular time for guests, with special worship and theological reflection times.

● In May, for three or four weekends, Lutheran youth groups from the Northwest come on retreat.

Solitude days are inserted four times between October and May. These are 24-hour periods (from Vespers to Vespers) in which the whole Village community takes time for individual contemplation, and most group activity and interpersonal verbal communication are suspended.

## Strains and Joys

Winter community normally averages 50 to 70 people, swelling to 100 or more for the weeks around Christmas, the January interim, Easter weekend, and other group retreat times. Thus, the size of the winter community is but a small fraction of the 350 to 425 who are present in the summer. And that creates a distinctly different dynamic.

Deeper relationships develop during the winter, since there are fewer people to know and most of them stay much longer than in the summer. "The community is built most profoundly by the winter months," says John Schramm.

Ellen Gamrath notes that "there is little distinction between guests and staff in the winter. And as a guest one is drawn into the working community of the Village much more than in the summer."

Another difference is that in the winter the same staff people tend to be doing both the management of Village operations and the leading of program. During the summer a separate teaching staff is available.

The winter community has been likened to an extended family. And that reality can put a strain on nuclear family life.

"Dual commitments, to the larger but still-intimate community and to one's immediate family, can be difficult for some of us to balance," says Elmer Witt.

To let individual families have some time by themselves, the Village for about the past decade has scheduled one take-out evening per week in the winter. Food is prepared communally in the Village kitchen but families are free to take it for eating in their living space and, except for a brief worship time, no activities are scheduled for that evening.

There are other reasons for tension in the winter community. Because the group is so small, one's absence from any activity is noticed immediately, and such absences can quickly build resentments. In a tight and intimate community such as Holden in winter, anonymity is not possible.

Yet, people also need time to be alone. The overnight trail outings of summertime are not much of an option when the snow is eight feet deep. The day of solitude every couple of months is one attempt to provide time for the individual.

"We struggle to find a balance between our work and our growth as persons," says Elmer Witt. "The community provides the days of solitude and the free evenings in order to allow time for our personal development, theologically and spiritually."

"In the winter we do need to work harder at maintaining relationships," says Barbara Rossing, Village associate pastor from 1986 to the present. "But our worship life in winter community is what we depend on to keep us healthy. There is much more sense of continuity in worship than we can ever hope to achieve in the summertime."

## Whose Village Is It?

"In the summer you can get away from people you'd rather not relate to," notes Gertrude Lundholm. (She began coming to Holden with her husband Beanie, an Augustana College, Illinois, music professor, in 1963. Beanie, who died in 1984, was father of the Beanie-sings after evening meals.) "But in the winter it's like a family: you have to deal with confronting one another."

Gertrude also notes that winter community residents "have to resist becoming possessive about the Village. It's easy for winter Villagers to think that Holden belongs to them—and that those summer one-week visitors are outsiders." Those who agree with Gertrude are not fond of the term "guest" and would prefer that all Holden participants be known simply as "Villagers."

Mentioned earlier were some of the kinds of Holden activity that can happen only in the October-to-May kind of community. There are others. In the early 1970s, a winter habit of elegant progressive dinners, moving from chalet to chalet, was begun. Later, when Paul Hinderlie was running the kitchen, the cooks on an occasional winter evening would prepare a fancy-restaurant setting, complete with menus, candlelight, soft music, and finely attired servers. (Paul, a son of Mary and Carroll, now operates Harbor View Cafe, a quality restaurant in Pepin, Wisconsin.)

The winter gathering place is Koinonia, which since its expansion in the early 1980s has had a kitchen and dining room adequate for the winter community. Nearly all worship, program discussions, and other aspects of community life are conducted in Koinonia. Unusual recreation possibilities, beyond cross-country skiing and snowshoeing and making of "snowpersons," mark the winter as well. Gertrude Lundholm speaks of Christmas seasons when the Jacuzzi whirlpool was kept open. If you ask her in the right way, she may be willing to show you "a picture of myself in bathing suit and snowshoes."

## A Place for Healing

The winter Holden is, more than the summer, a community for people in transition, a refuge for those seeking a healing time and place.

"Those who are between jobs, or dealing with the death of a loved one, or reeling from a divorce or some other kind of traumatic change in life situation—many such people find the winter community a place of grace and special healing," says Elmer Witt. "We are able to provide a helpful ministry to many. Unfortunately, because of the particular intimacy of this community, we sometimes also have to say No to certain kinds of troubled persons. We simply don't have the professional competence here to help the most seriously distressed people."

At its best, the winter Holden is a community of people who become united in one vocation. All work with a single vision and will to accomplish what needs doing.

Dale Moultine, Village fire chief since 1986, mentions the collating parties as an example. "When there is a mailing to go out to the 20,000 names on the Holden list, we gather the whole community to get it done, and it's a fun time. The Village in winter is sort of like a traditional family farm—the whole family is together in all aspects of life."

# 6 The Village Runs On Volunteers

*It's not that any of it seems like work. It's just that there's so darn much of it!*
*—Werner Janssen, Holden business manager 1963-84, on making the Village operational in the 1960s*


Operating Holden Village requires many skilled people, including both long-term staff and shorter-term volunteers. It also requires ingenuity, brashness, and luck.

It is no simple matter to maintain a comfortable living community for 400 people in a wilderness setting. Everything they need must be made in the Village or brought in from a distant outside world. Seeing that it all comes together is the Village staff, and the key person for day-to-day operations is the business manager.

Supervising Village operations for nearly 21 of its years as a retreat center was Werner Janssen, who served as business manager from November 1963 until the fall of 1983, then gave another year as part-time management consultant. Others in the Village management role have been Gil Berg (1961-63), Roger Ockfen (1984-86), and Kent Burgess (since 1987).

"In the early years, we didn't know what was not possible, so we did it anyway," says Werner Janssen. "It also helps if you're just a bit naive."

## The Staff

During the early 1960s Holden was able to afford very few paid staff. That category expanded somewhat, especially in the

1980s, and today some 20 positions are considered long-term (commitment of a year or more) and nearly all of these are compensated, though usually on a stipend that is well below market rates. (They also receive room, board, and health coverage.) In addition to director and business manager, these positions include staff coordinator, registrar, bookkeeper, associate pastor, administrator/operations manager, program associate, chief carpenter, electrician/hydro manager, chief cook, mechanic, plumber, store manager, fire chief, resource center director, and chief driver. Some of the positions are half-time.

All other Holden workers are volunteers, serving a minimum of three weeks. In the summer there may be as many as 110 short-term staff in the Village at a time. Holden simply could not function without them, and it has been that way from the beginning.

Volunteers must find their own way to and from the Village. They usually work six-hour days, six days a week, though flexibility allows volunteers to take advantage of the opportunity for hiking and attendance at sessions. As pay, they receive room and board, plus access to Holden's program riches and its community life.

"The only time I pushed our volunteers was when they didn't collect their pay; that is, when they refused to take time to go to discussions," says Carroll Hinderlie. "I used to tell them that Holden wasn't mining copper any more, but we were still at Holden to mine some of God's other riches."

Chris Bekemeier, staff coordinator since August 1985, says, "I often marvel at the way volunteers keep popping up like little miracles just when we need them, letting the ministry of Holden continue." A volunteer herself in 1977, 1978, and 1984, Chris notes that "Holden volunteers have always been a source of friendship, joy, support, and empowerment to me.

That's a major reason why I've kept coming back and why I love my present job."

Traditionally, most volunteers have been college-age young adults. From the early years, large numbers of students on summer break came from such Lutheran schools as St. Olaf, Pacific Lutheran, Valparaiso, Augustana of Illinois, and California Lutheran. While the majority of volunteers are in their 20s and early 30s, a significant number of retired persons have served from the earliest years, and recently a growing number of couples in their mid-life years have been volunteering.

A retired barber from Colville, Washington, Hortie Christman, was among the first of the retiree volunteers. Carroll Hinderlie calls him "the patron saint of Holden volunteers." Hortie first came with his wife Mary in 1965 and over the next eight years they filled a variety of staff roles at the Village.

"Hortie was a Christ-like figure: no pomp, non-judgmental, full of grace," says Carroll. "He asked all the right questions. Mary also was a great gift to the Village, a person of grace seasoned with salt and much wisdom and humor. She learned New Testament Greek while at Holden." Hortie died in 1973; Mary still lives in Colville.

Other older volunteers who served over many seasons were Al Swihart and Omar Cline. Both made major contributions to Village landscaping and keeping of the grounds.

## "It Could Not Operate Without You"

Still, most Holden volunteers are young and single. It is as though the early vision of Holden as a young adult center was fulfilled in an unexpected way. While not developing a program orientation for young adults, Holden certainly became a place where they could serve—and could probe their faith commitments. For people of all ages, but especially for young adults,

Holden has always been a primary place for testing one's love-hate relationship with the church, in a setting where the church would not spurn the tester.

"Holden helped me to discover that spoon-fed Christianity would never cut it for me," says Dave Michel, a three-month summer volunteer in 1978 who returned for stints in 1980 and 1981-82. "It gave me a deepened understanding of my commitment to the gospel."

The Village also serves, for some young adults, as a community of support where they can test the values of their culture and the policies of their government. Mark Lundholm, who was in his late teens during the early Vietnam War years, says, "Holden gave some of us the permission to question whether our government was doing the right things."

For not a few of its thousands of young-adult volunteer alumni, Holden continues to occupy a central place in their identities. Ann Hafften, who spent five months in 1974 as postmistress, puts it this way: "When people today ask me who I am, the fact that I spent time as a volunteer at Holden is something I always mention as foundational. I was 21 when I went there and had just finished college at a non-Lutheran school. Holden was a way of recovering my identity in the Lutheran family."

Ann returned as a volunteer in 1976 and 1979 and is now a member of the Holden board. She thinks a big part of Holden's impact on volunteers is that they are made to feel very important. "Carroll Hinderlie told us repeatedly, 'This place could not operate without you.' We always knew we were essential to the functioning of the Village. That's probably why it was simply not cool to do anything but work hard, which is what we did."

The Village was also a setting for many youthful volunteers to explore life work options. Gertrude Lundholm notes that "experiences at Holden have helped many volunteers to find their occupations—cooks, carpenters, science people, even firefighters, as well as clergy and others in the humanities."

Carol Nolte, one of the early volunteers and later a Holden board member, believes there may be dozens who decided to become pastors after working at Holden, and includes herself in that number.

Many lasting friendships have been formed among Holden volunteers, and a number of marriages have resulted from relationships established there.

## From Holden to the World

Quite a number of volunteers have gone from Holden to volunteer service with the church internationally. Among them have been Karen Bustad, Andy Hinderlie, Doris and Art Holste, Marlayne Johnson, Carol Nolte, Ruth Odde, Meredith Olson, Jane Rossing, Mary Ann Teske, and Wanda Thykeson.

The reverse is true as well: returning overseas missionaries have gone to work at Holden. Two recent examples are June Prange and Carolyn Schurr, who spent a couple of years on long-term staff after service to the church in Papua New Guinea.

Holden has often inspired volunteers to explore other parts of the world. For Ann Hafften, it was Holden's "emphasis on community which led me to investigate the kibbutz movement in Israel."

While the minimum volunteer service is one three-week period, some Holden volunteers return annually, really functioning as permanent staff, though without compensation. One of these is Dorothy Bennett, who established the lapidary shop, equipped it herself, has managed it for two decades, and has also taught class sessions. Another was Fern Olson, long-time leader of housekeeping.

Through 1963, volunteers were recruited by the national Lutheran youth offices. Since the summer of 1964 that function has been handled by the Village itself. Volunteers must be at least 18. In applying, they agree to "strive to create and maintain an atmosphere within the community which will supplement and support the ministry and purpose of Holden." They also accept Holden's disciplines, including:

- attendance at staff meetings
- attendance at evening Vespers and Sunday Eucharist
- participation in Village programs, as time permits
- a desire to serve and to practice hospitality toward staff and guests of the Holden community
- willingness to live under two Holden policies (which are also laws of Washington state): no drinking of alcoholic beverages if under age 21; no use of non-medical drugs

## It's Not All Work

Among the many work areas available to volunteers are the hike haus, lawns and landscaping, carpentry, Narnia (children's program), the museum, kitchen, waiting tables, crafts, driving buses and maintenance vehicles, housekeeping, snack bar, logging, sawmill, tape ministry, garbology, library, and assisting the lapidarist, mechanic, registrar, recreation director, or in the resource center—and more. Further, all Holden volunteers are trained to respond to Village fire alarms.

But not all is work for Holden volunteers. They are encouraged to take time for day-long and overnight hikes, and to participate in Village learning sessions. They have also developed a tradition of creative contributions to the community's life in play, worship, and the arts.

Matins, a brief reflection on the Word of God following breakfast each morning, is the responsibility of volunteer staff, and they often provide leadership for Vespers. Their offerings in music and drama benefit the entire Village family. Volunteers take part in discussions as their schedules permit, most noticeably in evening forums. They also have an early morning Bible study daily.

Their most visible gift outside of work assignments, however, could be their contribution to the whimsy of the Village. Volunteers seem to take the lead in keeping Holden hilarity alive and well. They may offer original song lyrics and a dance line at mealtime, or a spontaneous celebration in the Village Center after Vespers.

The biggest day each summer for volunteers is probably July 4th, when they provide most of the energy and creativity for the parade, the games, the children's boat race, and the evening talent show. In addition, most of them have at least part of their regular work to do on that day.

## Village Offices

From 1961 through 1965 the management of Holden was based in the Village only during the summer months. From about Labor Day to mid-May, since there was no winter community at the Village, it made sense to operate from an office in Seattle. The office was initially located in the second story of Gil Berg's business in the Ballard community, then for a few years it was in an office building owned by Gethsemane Lutheran Church. After people began staying through the winters at the Village in 1966, the office was moved there permanently, though for a couple of years in the late 1960s a telephone service was maintained in Chelan as well.

The first large physical undertaking at the Village itself was to get the buildings ready for use. That meant, first, cleaning them. Work campers in the summers of 1961 and 1962 assumed that task.

"I have memories of how makeshift everything was those early summers," says Carol Nolte. "There were mice everywhere, and lots of dirt."

Electrical power was not always available, either. Initially, the Village relied on diesel power for electricity. During the first summers, it was turned off around 10 p.m. Throughout the summer of 1963, which was unusually cool and damp at Holden, there was no heat or hot water in the living units. Village living was quite primitive.

"In those first years, nobody came to Holden because of comfort," says Werner Janssen. "What they got was really a camping experience that happened to be indoors."

The hydroelectric system was ready by 1964. That was also the year the first snow vehicle was acquired, a gift of Bill and Louise Pihl. Winter Village custodians now had transportation to and from Lucerne.

After the buildings were cleaned up in 1961 and 1962, they were useable. But it took several more years before all the buildings could be renovated. "We had that basically finished by 1966," Janssen recalls.

Werner at one point in the early 1960s spoke to the board about the task of getting the Village ready, when it seemed everything needed to be done at once. "It's not that any of it seems like work," he said. "It's just that there's so darn much of it!"

A major project was the rebuilding of one lodge into the present Koinonia. Willis Schellberg, an architect from Forest City, Iowa, who had visited Holden, designed the remodeling. It was carried out by volunteer labor between 1964 and 1966. The new section at the back was added in 1980-81 to provide for winter food service and additional summer education space.

"There has never been a plan to expand the capacity of Holden," says Janssen, "except perhaps to rebuild Chalet Two.

It's the right size now for program effectiveness and logistical support. To give it larger capacity would bring in a completely different dynamic."

## Holden Food

One of the major management challenges at Holden is food. Nearly everything to be eaten must be imported from down-lake. It has never proved practical to grow food in the Village. The weather is the chief problem, since the growing season is only about 50 days, with frost usually until late June and again as early as August. Attempts have been made to grow some vegetables, but they always seemed to become deer and chipmunk food before they could be delivered to the tables of people.

Because all the food raw materials have to be shipped in, a low-waste policy developed early. That policy extends to packaging as well. Glass and plastic containers are not popular items in the Village. Food or other materials that come only in glass or plastic are generally avoided—and guests who bring in glass or plastic are asked to pack them back out again. The goal is to recycle everything, and food waste goes back to the soil.

Wholesome food was part of the Holden philosophy from the outset. Today, the cooking leans toward vegetarian cuisine, with perhaps a couple of red-meat meals each week, a couple with fish, and a heavy emphasis on whole grains, pastas, legumes, dairy products, and tofu. Refined-sugar desserts are a rarity. But the snack bar in the Village Center provides sweets during its open hours each afternoon and evening.

Whole-grain breads, baked daily, are a Holden trademark. Wheat is ground in the Village and leftovers are added as available: cooked cereals, egg whites, pureed vegetables, oat bran, soy flour. Holden bread is a hearty product. It also becomes the staple for hikers' lunches.

The first head cook was Bertha Pearson. She prepared food for work campers and guests the summer of 1961 on a fireplace that was found in the miners' village and set up on three legs behind Chalet One. It can be seen today at the Portal Museum.

Eventually the cooking moved into the present dining hall and Bertha continued as chief cook for several more summers. Beginning in 1963 she also served for a decade or more as cook at Seattle's Lutheran Bible Institute during the school year, returning as Holden's summer cook through 1968.

In the early 1970s, Village cooks moved aggressively into cooking most items from scratch. Among the head cooks who have championed simple, nutritious foods featuring proteins other than meats have been Paul Hinderlie, Stan Sivesind, Will Mowchan, David Christian, and Tim Kieschnik. Both Paul and Stan have entered food service professions.

## Food, Politics, and Fun

Food is something of a political statement at Holden. Not only does it speak of simplicity and the wisdom of eating low on the food chain, food also expresses approval or disapproval of certain political realities in the world. During the time of the Nestle boycott aimed at changing that company's infant-formula marketing practices, no Nestle product dared enter the Village. Today, coffee is bought from a cooperative in Nicaragua. And all food products are purchased, whenever possible, directly from producers.

Food questions seem to be part of every board agenda. What is Holden's responsibility to model good nutrition habits in its food service? How close to vegetarian should the Holden diet be? How compromising is it to be catering to Villagers' sweet tooths in the snack bar? At the 1982 annual meeting, the board discussed a motion to remove salt shakers from tables in the dining hall, on the grounds that diners were harming themselves by adding too much salt to the food. The motion was defeated, though narrowly.

Food, as with everything at Holden, is also an occasion for celebration and humor. The cooking staff and waitri (non-sexist Holden term for servers) like to announce a meal of leftovers as "the week in review." Witty new songs about food appear in a continuing stream. Guests join the food fun too, like the man some years ago who on July 4th wore a sandwich board reading, "I came as a Lutheran—I leave as a lentil."

One of the best food stories comes from the Paul Hinderlie era. For a Sunday Eucharist, Paul had baked bread with a particularly hard crust. It was so hard that when it came time in the service for the bread to be shared the celebrant, Fritz Norstad, found it impossible to break the loaf. Fritz believes to this day that it was made so intentionally. In any case, after several attempts to crack the loaf by hand, a frustrated Fritz broke it over his knee as if it were a stick of kindling.

Within seconds the congregation was singing, "Let us break bread together, on our knees," and roaring in laughter.

## Financial Support

Fees charged to Holden guests have always been modest. The weekly charge of $50 per adult in 1963 has grown to $150 in 1987—not quite keeping pace with the dollar's decline in value over the quarter century. The weekly fee for youth ages 13-18 is currently $100, for ages 4-12 $60, and for those under 4 it is $30. The maximum weekly charge for a family, regardless of size, is $540. A reduced adult charge of $120 per week is offered to retired persons in the September through May period, and the same rate is available to pastors and spouses from October through May.

Fees alone have never paid the full cost of Village operations, if the value of volunteer labor is figured in. In the first decade or so, perhaps as much as 50% of the operating costs was covered by the in-kind gift of volunteer labor and by money gifts, from guests and others. Today, the subsidy is more like 25%.

The current annual operating budget is approximately $1,000,000. That includes nearly $100,000 in gift income and a calculation of $200,000 as the value of donated labor.

At least one standard line item is not present in the Holden budget: there is no expenditure for fire insurance. "We never insured against fire because the rates would have been prohibitive," says Janssen. "We therefore provide all of our own fire security, which is why we have such strict rules about smoking." (At Holden they ask that smoking be limited to the porches of residences, the pool hall, and the patio outside the dining hall.)

Holden had major financial problems in its first decade, and Carroll Hinderlie devoted much of his time as director to fundraising. Still, the Village has always taken a rather relaxed attitude toward long-term financial planning. "We resisted forming an endowment or a foundation, and the Village has never used professional fundraisers," says Carroll.

"Holden has never been in debt," says Werner Janssen. "We never had to borrow money because friends of the Village always came through when we asked for help."

## Werner's Auctions

One way they were asked was via auctions conducted by Werner, to raise money for specific needs. Mary Hinderlie remembers them as "marvelous times—they not only raised money but were also occasions of great fun."

Sometimes the Village has benefited from the generosity of a few people to a major project. An example would be the Jacuzzi whirlpool, given in the early 1970s by Ernie and Marvin Gulsrud and Fern Olson, all of whom had Spokane roots.

In 1987 Holden launched a three-year capital fund drive, seeking support for several projects, among them improving the stability of the hydroelectric system, vehicle replacement, completing the Portal Museum, resurfacing the Lucerne to Holden road as required by the Forest Service, completion of the new sewer system, remodeling of the Narnia building for expanded use as an educational and social facility, and possible rebuilding of Chalet Two. The board is also giving consideration to launching a deferred-giving program.

Village participants and friends have always been generous. That is clear. So have the thousands of volunteers. Without people giving both money and work time to Holden, it is fair to say there would be no Holden.

**PERMANENT DIRECTORS.** Carroll Hinderlie, 1963-77, with Mary (above) celebrating their 35th wedding anniversary, July 9, 1974, at Holden. JOHN SCHRAMM, 1978-84, with Mary Schramm (below left). ELMER WITT (in jacket), 1984-present, with U.S. Senator Paul Simon of Illinois and 1986 theme plaque.

gentle
justice
1986

**WES PRIEB** (above) stands outside pool room, his summer domain (Nancy Anderson photo).

**WINTER** at Holden means heavy snowfall on chalets and Railroad Creek footbridge. (Charles Lutz photos).

**ULY FOURTH** parade atchers in 1983 (center photo, om left) were Tim Lutz, AELC astor (and later Bishop) Will erzfeld, and Duane Lansverk, ho now chairs Holden board lertha Lutz photo). MISS BERTY look-alikes, July 4, 86, were Director Elmer Witt d Pastor Barb Rossing, olden associate pastor.

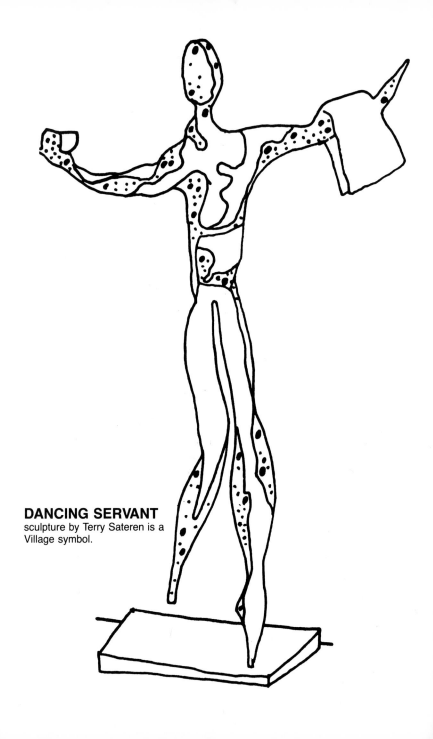

**DANCING SERVANT**
sculpture by Terry Sateren is a Village symbol.

# 7 A Fragile, Spectacular Setting

*I have never been any place where, from the moment I arrived, I felt so completely apart from the world and where I could so clearly see the world from which I had come and to which I would return. It's not getting away from it all; it's really getting back to it all, back to the basics of one's existence.*

—*Wilton Bergstrand, Augustana Lutheran Church youth director in the early 1960s and a major promoter of Holden Village*

Holden Village has a physical setting which is at once its great glory and its chief challenge.

No one disputes that the mountain beauty is a feast for the eyes. But the constant accompaniment to Holden's spectacular natural remoteness, unspoiled (mostly) by human interference, is the fact of wilderness. And life for a sizeable human community in wilderness is difficult and demanding.

In addition, there is the challenge posed to wilderness environment by what is left from the mining operation. The tailings in particular are a scar on God's creation for which healing and restoration have not been found.

How does Holden live in harmony with its physical surroundings? How does it utilize its setting as a program opportunity, teaching Villagers of both the magnificence and the fragility of wilderness?

97

## The Setting as Teaching Tool

From Holden's first summer as a retreat center the physical setting has been central to the learning that occurs there. The 1961 program weeks planned by Seattle's Lutheran Bible Institute featured study of God's revelation in both the Bible and the creation. Hiking into the mountains and fishing in the lakes and streams was also part of the experience for work campers and others who came that summer. The glacial and geological features of the area, plus the mine history, have provided additional teaching elements from the first. Each is a reminder of the gifts of creation which Holden represents.

Today, a guest during a typical week-long visit is able to sample the following:

1. *Hiking*. Hikes at Holden come in great diversity—strenuous to easy, short to long, from an hour to several days. The staff at the hike haus is ready to help with counsel, with rental of equipment, and with trail lunches. The lunches require advance reservations, as do hikes into the nearby Glacier Peak Wilderness, since there is a limit to the number who are allowed on its trails at one time. Here is a list of the more popular hikes:

● Short nature hike between the Village and Railroad Creek, led by Gertrude Lundholm frequently during the summer; takes less than an hour. Gentle walk.

● "Hello Holden" hike. Follows road to location of Winston Camp, former miners' homesites; about one-third mile. Self-guiding with booklet by Evelyn Streng available in bookstore.

● Mine hike, across Railroad Creek to mine site and Portal Museum; led by Rudy Edmund or people he has trained, regularly in summer; takes about two hours. (The bookstore offers *The Mine*, Rudy's summary of the mine history.)

● Ten-mile Creek Falls. Parallels road toward Lucerne, two miles roundtrip, about one hour, easy walk.

• Honeymoon Heights. Climbs 1500 feet to location of miners' housing from 1920s, two miles, about two hours, average difficulty.

• Copper Basin. Rises 2300 feet to basin between Buckskin and Copper Mountains, five miles, at least four hours, strenuous.

• Domke Lake. Climbs 2000 feet above Lucerne to excellent fishing lake. Popular for overnights. Average difficulty.

• Hart Lake. Nine-mile roundtrip paralleling Railroad Creek to the west, elevation of 700 feet, four hours, average.

• Holden Lake. Climbs 2100 feet to glacial lake below Bonanza Peak (northwest of Village), 10-mile roundtrip, five to six hours, strenuous but worth the effort.

• Lyman Lake. Beyond Hart Lake, 18-mile roundtrip, 2400-foot climb, strenuous. Overnight recommended.

• Cloudy Pass. West of Lyman Lake, 20 miles roundtrip, 3200-foot climb, strenuous. Overnight recommended.

• Image Lake. Still farther west, 36-mile roundtrip, 3200-foot climb, strenuous. Two overnights recommended.

*Trails of Holden,* a guide to most of these trails and others, with maps, can be purchased at the bookstore.

2. *Fishing.* Licenses for fishing in Railroad Creek and the lakes are on sale in the Village store. All the fish in the streams and lakes belong to the trout family. Prevalent are cutthroat (note the vivid red color of the throat) and rainbow (note the color spectrum from head to tail). A narrated slide presentation on fishing at Holden is offered at the Portal Museum.

Cleaned fish may be delivered to the kitchen and the staff will prepare and serve it at breakfast the next day.

3. *Slide Presentations.* Lectures on the natural history of the Holden area, with slides, are presented several times each week in the summer. Among the offerings are introductions to Holden's glaciers, its flora and fauna, its four seasons, and the

mine, plus illustrated lectures on volcanoes, fossils, and the origins of mountains, continents, and ocean basins.

4. *Discussions*. Hour-long sessions on various topics related to the created world are also offered. Depending on who is available as a resource, the subject matter may range from Holden environmental challenges to the care of the wilderness to the ethics of hunting to seeking energy self-reliance for the Village to the relationship between science and biblical faith to the role of the Forest Service to the history of the mine to the importance of pets for human wellness to an exploration of creation theology. Nighttime star studies with telescopes are also offered on occasion.

5. *Book Seminars*. Both the bookstore and the library have good collections on the theology of creation, stewarding of the earth, and the natural history of the Glacier Peak Wilderness area. Book discussions can normally be arranged according to the interests of guests. Special Holden-related nature publications in the bookstore include (in addition to those mentioned above) *Critters of Holden* by Ernie Zoerb, *Wildflowers, Trees, and Shrubs of Holden Village* by Barbara J. Collins, and *The Holden Mine* by Nigel B. Adams.

## A Museum for the Village

The mine (whose history is discussed in Chapter Two) continues to be very much a part of Village life and lore. Its entrance tunnel into Copper Mountain was closed to the public in 1962 because it was a major safety hazard. But Village arrivals are aware of the mine's presence from their first glimpse of the tailings, even before they view the Village itself. Holdenites are reminded of the mine whenever they see the remains of the mine structures across Railroad Creek. And much of the mine history is preserved and displayed in the Portal Museum.

The museum was the dream of Rudy Edmund from the first summer he spent at the Village, when he found mammoth assortments of mine records and memorabilia. Officially designated by the Holden board as curator of the museum, Edmund is a professional geologist who has been on a personal crusade during the past quarter-century to safeguard, organize, and display the mine's artifacts for present and future generations.

"From my first walk through the mine buildings in 1962, I knew the records left behind by the Howe Sound Company had to be collected and preserved," says Rudy. "It also seemed logical that a place be found where selected materials could be on display so that all who came to Holden could learn about the mine from its early beginnings to its 1957 closing."

Rudy mentioned his concern to Gil Berg and Wilt Bergstrand in 1962. They invited him to return and spend the next summer working on the mine materials, which he did. Edmund and a volunteer work crew composed of Carol Nolte, Peter Lund-holm, Jan Edmund, Linda Edmund, and Nancy Leaf sorted through materials in all of the mine buildings and by the end of summer 1963 had boxes full of items moved to the potato room in the basement of the dining hall. They also prepared simple displays and opened a modest museum in the mine's change-house basement.

By 1965, as a dormitory was being remodeled into the present Koinonia, a museum was opened in the space now occupied by the circulating library. This area served for only a few years, then was taken for other purposes and the museum materials were again stored in the dining hall basement.

Meanwhile, at the urging of Rudy Edmund, Luvern Rieke, and Werner Janssen, the board agreed to transfer the official Howe Sound Company mine records to the archives of the University of Washington in Seattle. The transfer was accomplished in the fall of 1968 by Nigel Adams, who had been raised at Holden in its mining days and in his doctoral dissertation provides the historical account up to 1938 when the large-scale mining operation began.

When the resort buildings at Lucerne were given to Holden in 1977, the school house at Lucerne was envisioned as a location for the mine museum. It was the board's feeling that a general public of day-trippers on Lake Chelan, most of whom would never be guests at Holden, could then enjoy learning of the mine and seeing its artifacts. But when the Forest Service turned down Holden's proposal for the Lucerne site (see Chapter Eight), this museum plan died also.

## The Portal Opens at Last

By this time Holden had a science and technology committee, which joined in advocating for a permanent museum. The board in 1981 approved plans for construction of a museum building on the site of Howe Sound's assay house (built in 1937), making use of the original foundation and concrete floor. An architectural plan submitted by Dan Dierks was approved; it incorporated these features: a view of the Holden mine mill to the east; a view of Bonanza Peak to the west; a view of the top of Martin Ridge to the north, and an entrance at the north. (There is hope of replicating the portal entrance to the main tunnel into Copper Mountain; this feature was scheduled for completion by summer of 1987.)

The Portal Museum was completed in the spring of 1983 and dedicated on the Fourth of July that year. It provides an introduction to the Holden heritage in three areas:

* The history of Railroad Creek Valley and the Northern Cascades. Models, maps, and audiovisual presentations offer the geologic story of glaciers and of the life forms that came to occupy the area.

* The history of the Holden Mine, 1887 to 1957. Artifacts and historical data are presented through pictures, newspaper accounts, and various mine relics.
* The history of the gift of the abandoned mine buildings and property to the Lutheran church, 1957 to the present. Letters, photographs, and news clippings tell the story of the past 30 years.

The Portal is open at scheduled hours daily in the summer and special sessions with staff are announced periodically. Rudy Edmund continues as curator and spends most of every summer at the Village, as he has since 1962.

## Science and Technology Committee

In 1975 the Holden board created a scientific advisory group (soon renamed the science and technology committee). The move coincided with concern over the energy crisis. Its agenda also included exploration of food production at the Village, the problem of pollution from the mine and the tailings, sewage disposal, and conservation of the local forest.

The committee continued for almost 10 years, until the close of the Schramm administration in 1984. Its major projects included:

● Experimenting with aquaculture, both with Railroad Creek water at Holden and in Lake Chelan at Lucerne. The former was dropped because pollution levels in creek water were too high; the Lucerne option died when the development proposal there was denied by the Forest Service.

● Exploration of alternate hydro locations at various places in the Railroad Creek Valley.

● Developing a forest management plan in cooperation with the Forest Service.

● Experimenting with carrier pigeons for communication with operations at 25-Mile Creek and Lucerne, eventually abandoned because martens broke into the pigeon house two years in a row and dined on the partly trained pigeons.

● Developing heat exchangers to conserve the heat of waste hot water in the kitchen and placing solar collector panels atop the hospital building.

● Annual review of new technologies that might serve to reduce costs at Holden and improve its service efficiency.

● Exhaustive survey and inventory of trees on Holden's mineral leases and development of plans for increasing wood sources for lumber and fuel.

● Study of remaining mineral potential of Holden's patented leases and recommendations to trustees of actions needed to keep the leases in force under federal requirements.

● Continuing emphasis on Christian stewardship, which spawned a study booklet titled *Sharing God's Gifts* by Rudy Edmund (Minneapolis: Augsburg, 1978).

Persons serving on the science and technology committee during the 1975-84 period included Leo Bustad (veterinary medicine, chair), Mark Adams (industrial chemist), Earl Anderson (pastor), Terrill Chang (energy specialist), Larry Collins (geologist), D. W. Dorn (energy specialist), Rudy Edmund (geologist), Al Halvorson (soil scientist), Dorothy Halvorson (nutritionist), Linda Hines (educator), Marion Jacobsen (nutritionist), Dave Larson (financial specialist), Bill Matheson (professional engineer), Jim Skrinde (sanitary engineer), and Ray Skrinde (hydraulic engineer). Werner Janssen, Village business manager, provided staff services to the committee, and Roger McLellan, a foundation executive, served it as a consultant.

## Tailings—Solutions Silly and Serious

The mine tailings cannot be ignored. They are the first evidence of human activity seen as visitors approach the Village by road. They are not legally Holden's problem, since they are the property of the U.S. Department of Agriculture (parent agency of the Forest Service). But in reality they are very much Holden's problem, because the Village lives in their shadow and their dust.

Most people consider them a visual blight on the landscape. Beyond that, they blow about when the wind is up. And the chemicals in them—cyanide among these—pollute downstream Railroad Creek.

Most visitors to Holden hear suggestions for getting rid of the tailings—and the more imaginative visitors try to dream up their own solutions. (Here, the reader is invited to pause and brainstorm for new options; the most creative ideas will be rewarded by mention in the next edition of this book.) Among the classic proposals are these:

• Package the tailings in 20-minute "egg timer" containers and sell them in the Village store as "Golden Holden Sermon Timers."

• Require visitors from Minnesota to carry home a 10-pound bagful for dumping in the open pits of their state's Mesabi Iron Range.

• Ask each Villager coming from farm country to bring in a shoebox full of good top soil for covering the tailings (not so silly an idea, if a way could be found to avoid erosion).

Indeed, serious solutions have mostly been a variation on the theme of getting vegetation to grow. For many years sewage effluent was pumped to the top of one pile and grasses did indeed grow there.

The most elaborate scheme was to address three environmental issues simultaneously by (1) moving sewage effluent to the tailings; (2) growing jerusalem artichokes in the sewage to control wind pollution and replace the gold color with some green; (3) using the artichokes to produce fuel alcohol for powering Village vehicles.

John Schramm recalls, "Werner Janssen and I had a hope that the Village could become free of any dependence on petroleum. Putting artichokes on the tailings, to make alcohol for our motors, was part of that dream." But the plan was never implemented. Another sewage solution was chosen by the Village and the effluent is no longer pumped to the tailings. Conservation efforts have, however, reduced annual consumption of diesel fuel from 40,000 gallons to 10,000, and an expanded hydro capability now being developed will help further.

From time to time there is talk of reprocessing the tailings to remove the mineral wealth, chiefly in the form of gold, that remains therein. The theory has been that,when the world price of gold is at or above $380 an ounce, it is economically feasible to remove the gold. Were such a program to be undertaken, a mining company could be required by the Forest Service to solve the tailings problem once and for all as part of an agreement to remove the gold.

Another long-term environmental problem at Holden has been sewage disposal. The original Village sewer system was constructed in the mid-1930s. By the early 1970s the Forest Service was asking that a plan be developed for improving it. In 1985-87, at a capital investment of some $400,000, the entire system was rebuilt, with new lines in the Village and new drain field in the area of the former Winston Camp to the west. An adequate plan for the recycling and disposal of solid wastes is still under study.

## And the Animals . . .

Wildlife at Holden is near at hand, another reminder that this is life in the wilderness. The forest animals seem to view the Village as a sanctuary, which indeed it is.

Visitors to Holden are especially delighted to discover deer roaming about as though the Village were theirs. These are mule deer and the salt lick between Chalets One and Three attracts them all through the summer. They also come to graze in Holden's lush, well-watered lawns and cultivated flower beds, and are often seen in the circle at the top of Chalet Road in the early mornings and early evenings. Ernie Zoerb writes of the deer habits in his booklet *Critters of Holden:*

> They spend the winter season down by Lake Chelan and then move up the valley with the retreating snow. Their range knows little limit as they make it up to the alpine regions. . . . Late May and early June the fawns are born. Several times, well-meaning persons have carried into the Village fawns that they thought were sick. Little did they know that when the doe leaves her young the little fellow beds down and doesn't move a muscle. . . . Under no circumstances should a fawn ever be touched!

But the most common Village creatures are the chipmunk and the ground squirrel. The latter is slightly larger. The chipmunk can be distinguished by a more pointed nose and stripes extending to the end of it. Zoerb credits the presence of these rodents to the stone masons who constructed the dry rock walls when the mining town was built, since those walls are the safe haven where chipmunks and ground squirrels live. They are photogenic and seemingly unafraid. They are also freeloaders extraordinaire. Zoerb notes that these little animals

> . . . have their supermarket within running distance—the loading dock for left-over goodies, and sometimes the door is open for a sneak raid into the hike haus and store. At the east end of the wall is the entrance to the pool room from whence comes forth old popcorn that . . . Wes brings out for chippie consumption. . . . Chipmunks have in each cheek a little pocket opening inside of the lip for carrying food. . . . One day I watched a chippie on the loading dock where departing guests had piled their luggage. In the side pocket of one piece the owner had put a package of M and M's, no doubt to enjoy a snack on the return boat trip. What this person did not know

was that chipmunks are a bit nosy and are not bound by the Seventh Commandment. I watched this chippie put half a pack of M and M's in his cheek pockets.

Holden asks Villagers not to feed the chipmunks and ground squirrels. They find plenty of food in any case, and it is not healthy for young children to think of them as pets. They are, despite appearances to the contrary, wild animals, and are known to harbor diseases and parasites. Looking and picture taking are fine—but don't touch.

Bears are not as friendly as chipmunks. They are seen in the Village only rarely, usually when someone has foolishly left food out as enticement. Villagers will occasionally see bears at the edge of the forest near hiking trails. Overnighters are strongly encouraged to follow hike haus counsel concerning storage of food.

Other animals often seen along the trails, especially in the higher elevations, are marmot and pika. Both are rodents, the former reaching two or three feet in length, the latter only seven inches.

There are also beavers at work in Railroad Creek. And, while they are seldom seen by the casual hiker, coyotes, cougar, martens, and wildcats live in the high Cascades. From the boat on Lake Chelan, sharp-eyed passengers sometimes spot mountain goats.

Finally, what about birds? Most Villagers have enjoyed watching the hummingbirds at the feeders scattered about various Holden porches. Also spotted in the Holden vicinity have been warblers, grosbeak, woodpeckers, sparrows, clark's nutcrackers, grouse, stellar jays, western tanagers, brown creepers, nuthatches, swallows, flycatchers, vireos, juncos, wrens, hawks, pine siskin, blackbirds, cowbirds, chickadees, wax wings, robins and other thrushes, dippers, and kingfishers. Bald eagles may be seen above the hills of Lake Chelan. Photos of many of the birds identified in the area are kept at the Portal Museum.

The best way to see Village birds is to go on an early-morning bird hike. One is offered periodically in the summer.

## "Back to the Basics"

Being at Holden is incomplete unless one finds again one's link to the rest of God's created order. For some it may come while viewing the deer and chipmunks in the Village. For some it will happen when meeting a marmot along the trail. For others it might occur during a discussion of God's grace revealed in the creation. It could even come, one imagines, by reflecting on the stars above the peaks of Buckskin and Copper on a clear night while luxuriating in the Jacuzzi.

Despite such hedonistic touches as the Jacuzzi, enough remains of the wilderness experience that most Villagers find Holden a good place, in Wilt Bergstrand's words, "to get back to the basics."

# 8 Relationships To Be Nurtured

*We weren't trying to be a model for the parish, but we hoped people from the parishes would be able to appropriate whatever they felt was nourishing for their living in Christ.*
*—Mary Hinderlie, Holden teacher and program leader, 1963-77*

Relationships with the world beyond the Village are vital to Holden's life. Two institutional relationships in particular—with the U.S. Forest Service and with organized church structures—are of central importance. This chapter will review that pair of relationships, then will look at the question of exporting Holden to the world outside.

## "Forest Service Takes Pride"

The Forest Service approved Lutheran Bible Institute as the original recipient group. When LBI sought a broader base, "Holden Village Incorporated" was formed, and the Forest Service approved that entity as well.

"We had to satisfy two sets of criteria," recalls Vern Rieke. "The Forest Service insisted that we have the financial capacity to operate. Second, they needed to be comfortable with the kind of program we would offer and to know that Holden would be open to anyone who wished to come."

The Forest Service owns the Village property and continues to have ultimate control over Holden. Legally, it could close the Village for a higher public use and order all the townsite buildings removed, though such an eventuality is considered highly unlikely.

Holden Village does own property, but it is on the mine side of Railroad Creek: 234 acres of patented mining claims and 10 acres of mill site, plus another 200 acres of non-patented claims. The 18 acres of townsite, and a fraction of an acre at the Lucerne landing, are leased from the Forest Service.

"The Forest Service is our landlord," says Werner Janssen. "The Village operates under a special-use permit and needs Forest Service permission to change anything, including the color of paint on the buildings."

The first special-use permit was issued in February 1961. The current one, issued in 1981, is for 20 years. The Village pays an annual fee to the U.S. government of $600.

The Forest Service/Holden Village relationship has been a mutually satisfying one. "All the folks we dealt with were very cordial during my time there," says former director John Schramm. "They had real pride that there was an effective cooperative arrangement between a government agency and a private group."

Janssen recalls that Forest Service people "liked to remind us that we at the Village, as we served our primarily church constituency, were also serving a part of their public, U.S. citizens and taxpayers. It's true also that we were helping the Forest Service quite a lot by taking over the townsite after the mine closed. It meant they did not have to tear it down and clean up the area, which would have been a costly enterprise."

Elmer Witt, the current director, notes that the Forest Service "deserves some of the credit for the effective running of the Village because of their supervision, counsel, and support over the years."

The Forest Service maintains a guard at Holden through the summer months. That person lives west of the townsite and is frequently in the Village to present programs for guests and to consult with Holden management.

## The Lucerne Proposal

In 1977 the operators of the resort at Lucerne (the Mike Griffin family, Lutheran Church—Missouri Synod people from Seattle) closed their business and gave the buildings to Holden. The Village conducted extensive study of possible uses of the property over the next two years. It developed a plan for a program different from Holden's, to serve a more general public, with an emphasis on arts and crafts. A self-supporting community of artists, each living at Lucerne for up to three years, would conduct a program there both for day-trip visitors from Chelan or Stehekin and for people who would stay for several days. Aquaculture, a restaurant, and a museum on the history of the region were among the proposed features.

Local Forest Service officials and people in Chelan strongly supported the Holden plan, but it was ultimately turned down by the regional Forest Service office in Portland. The speculation was that officials there were reticent to enter another venture with the same church group and questioned whether Holden could develop its plan successfully.

Chelan community leaders initiated an appeal to Forest Service headquarters in Washington, D.C., but the Portland decision was upheld there. The outcome was that, because the Village did not want to operate Lucerne as a traditional resort, Holden had to clear the buildings and let the land be reclaimed by wilderness. Holden no longer has any holdings at Lucerne except for a small waiting chalet and a parking area. The dock, rebuilt in 1971, is owned by the Forest Service, though Holden contributed both labor and funds for its construction.

The 11 miles of gravel road from Lucerne to Holden run through federal government land. By agreement with the Forest

Service, Holden has use rights to the road and must share in its maintenance.

The Forest Service, of course, also controls where and when timber may be cut on the lands surrounding the Village. With Forest Service approval, Holden is able to remove lumber from nearby lands for both construction and firewood. When Holden became a church operation a Swiss logging crew was at work in the vicinity. As they finished their work in 1969, one of the loggers, Karl Wyssen, carved and left as a gift to Holden the Swiss alpenhorn which is mounted in the dining hall.

## The Churches and Governance

Holden's relationship with the Lutheran church has been unusual from the first. It has obvious Lutheran identity—and equally obvious ecumenical commitment. Further, while maintaining a strong church connection, it has stayed structurally independent of institutional church control.

When Holden was received by the Lutherans, relationships were quickly established with the youth ministries of five national church bodies: the brand-new American Lutheran Church (whose constituting convention opened just a few days after the Howe Sound phone call to Wes Prieb); the Lutheran Free Church (which would later vote to join the ALC in 1963); the Augustana Lutheran Church and the United Lutheran Church (both in the final years of planning their 1963 merger into the Lutheran Church in America); and the Lutheran Church—Missouri Synod.

By the time of Hinderlie's arrival as director in the spring of 1963 the five had thus become three national Lutheran church bodies. And Holden immediately became something of a symbol of the ability of those three churches to work together nationwide.

Board restructuring in the early 1960s gave each of the three national youth departments the authority to name five members to the Village board, and there were several slots for advisory members, including one for Lutheran Bible Institute of Seattle. That pattern continued through the decade.

From the earliest days, there have been far more lay people than clergy on Holden's board; 65 of 91 board members serving between 1961 and 1987 have been lay. Only 20 of the 91 have been women; the first was Amalie Shannon of Billings, Montana, in 1963-64.

In 1972, revised articles of incorporation made the board self-perpetuating. The youth ministry connection was removed but a provision was included specifying that one board member from each of the three national Lutheran bodies should be chosen by the Village board and ratified by the national churches. Another board person for each of the three churches was to come from the Northwest and to be ratified by the respective church authority in that region. This pattern continues to the present. The Association of Evangelical Lutheran Churches, following its formation in 1976, similarly received national and regional slots on the board.

Though Holden has had no formal tie with a Canadian church body, Canadian Lutherans have been on the board for many years (there were two in 1987). A relationship with the Evangelical Lutheran Church in Canada is currently being explored.

The board also expanded its membership beyond the Lutheran family. In 1987, two of 30 board slots were occupied by non-Lutherans.

## Church Skepticism

Not all of the Lutheran establishment initially believed the Village was a great idea. Some leaders felt it would be a white elephant, one way or another becoming a financial millstone for the church. Others at first held rather deep suspicions about where its program emphasis and theology might go.

Carroll Hinderlie recalls that "there was a good deal of friction between Holden and the church in the early years; some church leaders did not want Holden to happen. And there were those who feared we were developing a new 'in' group at the Village. But gradually Holden was accepted."

Mary Hinderlie remembers that "at first some of the clergy did not like to come to Holden, when they found they tended to lose their pastoral prefix there—everybody became just human beings. But for many pastors, once they got used to it, that became Holden's great attraction for them. It was liberating to be at a place where name and work and station in life were of little importance, where you could meet people simply on the level of ideas."

Ellen Gamrath says, "Carroll had a strong conviction that Holden would not make it if it were taken over by the ecclesiastical establishment. He was determined to build a Village that was non-establishment, and he did. But that does not mean the Village is a renegade movement. It always has existed for the renewal of the parish."

Carroll believes that Holden's focus "needs to stay on the life of the parish." But he also concedes that the Holden community can never be like a normal parish. "A congregation's life must deal with everybody, while Holden's participants are self-selecting."

Holden should not try to be a model parish, says Mary Hinderlie, "but a place to celebrate all things, including difficulty. We hoped the parishes would benefit through people appropriating whatever they felt was nourishing to their living in Christ. We also sought in the 1960s to be a place where people could reflect on the structures of our U.S. society. We tried to provide acceptance for both those entering service in Vietnam and those who were draft resisters."

In net result, there can be no doubt that Holden Village is a ministry of the church. It provides ministry in a rich variety of ways for those who participate in the life of the Village, whether as guests or as staff. It also equips the people of God for their own ministries in home communities and throughout the world when they leave.

## Church Differences

Holden was destined to be a crucible for the debates swirling among Lutherans in North America during the past three decades.

On the one hand, the Village as a non-establishment expression of Lutheran community was able to live out a unity that was not yet present at more official levels. On the other hand, as an inter-Lutheran venture it was a locus where inter-Lutheran differences were bound to surface. Most apparent have been the differences between the Lutheran Church—Missouri Synod and the rest of the Lutherans. Two concerns have proved to be the most difficult: inter-Lutheran celebration of the Eucharist and the role of ordained women.

In the first years, the Village did not celebrate the Lord's Supper officially. "Secret Communions were the result," says Carroll Hinderlie, "groups going off to have the Sacrament privately, outside the Village worship center. It was clear we could not continue that. When we began having open Communion services, some Missouri Synod people questioned it, since LCMS was not in official fellowship with the other Lutherans. I remember that the first Missouri pastor to celebrate the Eucharist at Holden was Paul Heyne. But some of the ALC and LCA people also questioned our offering Communion, because we had no congregation at the Village in those days."

The matter of congregational sponsorship of the Eucharist was resolved technically for a time by doing it in the name of the ALC's Lake Chelan Lutheran Church in Chelan. Later, Fullness of God congregation was organized at the Village (see next chapter).

Carol Nolte recalls that "Holden was one of the first places in the nation where Lutherans of various groups were regularly communing together. Young children were also admitted to Communion there before it became the general practice in U.S. Lutheranism."

The other issue, probably even more divisive, involves the leadership role of ordained women at Holden. Both the ALC and the LCA began ordaining women in 1970. Holden has since had three women on its staff as pastors. Their leadership in worship, particularly their presiding at the Eucharist, has been a matter of distress to some LCMS people.

At the same time, says Ellen Gamrath, "Holden has also provided an avenue for LCMS women to serve." Ellen and another LCMS woman, Betsy Nagel, became the first women on the reorganized board in 1972, and served for 14 and 12 years respectively. Ellen believes "the Village really became a refuge for many victims of LCMS political change after 1969. And I think the reason official LCMS never fussed very much about what happened at Holden was that the Village was seen as ALC-dominated and not formally tied to the national churches anyway."

## Exporting the Village

Can Holden Village be taken outside the Village? Holdenites have always carried home ideas and ways of doing things which became meaningful to them at Holden. And in the early years the Holden community would occasionally go outside with a bit of the Village. Gertrude Lundholm recalls, "In the winter of 1969-70 we did a musical service in Chelan which was much appreciated."

But what of transporting a Holden-like experience permanently to another place? That question became increasingly important once it was apparent that there were people wanting to come to Holden between mid-June and late August who could not get in, and there was no feasible way of increasing Holden's capacity.

The Village articles of incorporation provide that "the work of the corporation shall be carried out at such locations as the trustees may designate." While several ways of exporting Holden have been considered over the years, none has been permanently established.

The earliest export proposal came in 1969, when the board considered a plan to open a winter program in Texas. The Village had no winter program at the time, but the Texas proposal was never developed. At about the same time, a proposal to operate a winter program in Hawaii was discussed but not pursued.

In June 1974 the board considered a plan to purchase and operate a farm. Three chief arguments for the idea were advanced: extension of Holden's ministry, food production for Village uses, and provision of a facility where staff could go for rest and relaxation. The board agreed that the idea should have more study.

A year later the board first learned of the possibility that the Lucerne resort facilities would be given to Holden. The gift was made reality in 1977 and it became the focus for Holden expansion talk during the next few years.

In the winter of 1981-82 an experiment led by Joel and Gretchen Oines was launched at 25-Mile Creek. Holden owns a seven-acre plot at 25-Mile, which is near the end of the road on the west side of the lake; until 1985 the Lake Chelan boat docked there. Joel and Gretchen had been on Holden staff since 1980 and had lived at Lucerne that summer, helping to develop the Lucerne proposal. They and several other young adults lived together at 25-Mile Creek from late in 1981, planted a garden in the spring of 1982, and developed a proposal for presentation to the board that June.

The proposal was called "Tekoa" (after the biblical village from which the prophet Amos came). Tekoa suggested that three possible locations for a Holden away from Holden be considered: one urban, one rural, and one at "Tekoa Landing," the 25-Mile Creek location. Three disciplines were to be central to the Tekoa concept for all sites—hospitality, community, and care of the earth.

The only one of the three sites ever pursued was Tekoa Landing, where Holden built a community building that would house six adults. The members of the community living there were expected to engage in demonstration agriculture projects and to manage Holden's car-parking and telephone service at 25-Mile Creek (later moved a few miles south to Field's Point, when a new parking facility and boat dock were opened there).

"Tekoa Landing was quite different from Holden in community feeling," says Joel Oines. "Holden is a wilderness setting, and isolated. Tekoa Landing was not—and that made it very different." The Tekoa Landing experiment was discontinued in 1985. The idea of operating a Holden away from Holden has been essentially dormant since. (The management of the parking lot and telephone service at Field's Point has been handled since then by a Holden staff couple, Beverly and Del Wolf.)

## Exporting Holden by Mail

The Village is being exported these days by other means. One is Holden's audiotape ministry. It began as early as 1963, when Armin Grams' summer lectures were recorded. The program was developed further by Donn and Dottie Rosenauer in 1967. Dave and Mary Carlson systematized it in 1969. In the 1970s the quality of the equipment was upgraded. Sieg Schroeder worked year-round with the tape ministry for some years in the late 1970s.

Today, audiocassettes of several thousand talks and discussions exist; they are displayed in the reference library in Koinonia. Villagers may listen to them at several locations in the Village, may purchase duplicates to take home, or may order them from catalogs that are mailed to them.

The Village opened a resource center in 1982, with Dan Erlander as first director. It offers exhibits to visitors and provides periodic mailing to those who subscribe via a voluntary contribution. Included are worship resources, Holden recipes, capsule book reviews and bibliographies, ideas for advocacy on current social issues, and varieties of news and notes.

Erlander, now a campus pastor at Pacific Lutheran University in Tacoma, also authored two studies while at Holden which have become popular for congregational use. *By Faith Alone: a Lutheran Looks at the Bomb* is a review of Christian peace ethics in a nuclear age. *Baptized We Live: Lutheranism as a Way of Life* looks at what is distinctive about the Lutheran movement within the church catholic. Each study provides curriculum for several sessions. They may be ordered from the Holden bookstore.

So, while not planted elsewhere, Holden does offer a variety of exports. And its preeminent export remains the people who have been Villagers—staff and guests alike—as they take home with them and transplant to their own communities the gifts of renewal they received at Holden.

# 9 Holden As Worshiping Community

*Holden Village is a worshiping community whose primary vocation is the ministry of hospitality, expressed in the hosting of some 5000 people a year.*
*—John Schramm, Holden director, 1978-84*

The calendar is important at Holden Village. The church's calendar, that is. The rhythm of the Village is determined by a cycle for worship that is annual, seasonal, weekly, and daily.

At Holden there's an exuberant commitment to the church year. And it's not just the seasons and major festivals we know from back home, but all those minor ones, too. Like Candlemas (not Groundhog Day) on February 2, and Holy Cross Day on September 14.

Furthermore, the commemorations in the front of Lutheran Book of Worship (pages 10-12) are posted at the start of each week throughout the year, and they give flesh and flavor to that week's prayer life in the community.

## Eucharist at the Center

The high point of each week is the celebration of the Eucharist. It has been weekly at Holden since July 4, 1965, well before many Lutheran congregations in America rediscovered weekly Communion. It happens on Sunday evening (the Sunday morning service is Matins) and it's a festival service every time.

The presiding minister is usually the Village director or the associate pastor. The proclamation is developed with the assistance of text study held earlier in the week, in which any members of the community may participate. There is usually special music by a choir and perhaps also by a vocal or instrumental soloist.

The passing of the peace is not your perfunctory 30-second drill at Holden. It may last more like 6 to 8 minutes and it becomes an occasion for repair of interpersonal relationships.

"You don't go to Communion angry or with a grudge; you deal with it during the sharing of the peace," says Ann Hafften, a former volunteer. "It's a time for reconciliation and forgiveness, which helps make Sunday night the high point of the week. It's both celebrative and healing."

The daily worship rhythm includes a morning word offered by one of the staff, following breakast. Evening Vespers is the one time each day that the entire community is expected to be together. Vespers may be formal or informal, led by a guest or a staff person. In summer, each week usually includes one Vespers led by the children from Narnia and one that is primarily music.

A practice of midday intercessions developed in Holden's early days. From Monday through Saturday, just before lunch, a group (usually from five to 20 people) gathered with Werner Janssen as the regular convenor. There was a specific theme for each day: Monday was given to concerns for the economy and for workers; Tuesday to culture and the arts; Wednesday to healing; Thursday to proclamation of the gospel; Friday to prayers for the church and its leaders; Saturday to global needs and world mission. "We decided that a retreat center could not run without daily times of prayer—morning, noon, and evening," says Carroll Hinderlie, Village director when the noon intercessions were begun. "Even those who couldn't join us, because of work or whatever, knew what we were praying about and in a sense could be with us."

Currently, the winter community prays each day for three specific former staff persons, and then sends them a card to inform them. "It's remarkably powerful as a way of uniting the Holden of the past with the Holden of the present," says Barbara Rossing, Village associate pastor since 1986.

## Laboratory for Worship

The Village has been giving leadership to the larger church in worship renewal for some time, functioning as a virtual laboratory for liturgical reform.

Many creative orders for various occasions have been written and tested at Holden. New settings for two of the daily liturgies have been composed by Village musicians: Matins by Tasche Jordan and Vespers by Marty Haugen. Both may be purchased through the Holden bookstore.

And the Holden community was struggling with the problem of gender in liturgical language long before that concern became a conventional matter in the English-speaking world.

Music in worship at Holden sets a high standard of excellence, without becoming fussy. Congregational singing is robust. Special music is always done well.

The worshiper in the Village Center is aware of the visual arts as well. Banners abound. Specific permanent features include the altar designed and built by Arnold Flaten and George Utech, the "Dancing Servant" statue sculpted by Terry Sateren, the painted chancel cross given by Christians in El Salvador, and the "Four Seasons of Holden" ceiling painted by Richard Caemmerer Jr. (A program introducing Caemmerer's painting is offered periodically during the summer.)

But not all is harmony in worship at Holden. While worship is certainly the chief glue for creating and sustaining community, is can also be a source for division. The problem is that Holden seeks simultaneously to be a place of openness to non-believers and agnostics and a worshiping community of Christian believers. It's hard to make the two mix. Even though applicants for volunteer positions are told of the Vespers attendance expectation, for example, some volunteers after coming to the Village occasionally have objected to it.

## Fullness of God Congregation

During its first decade the Village had no organized congregational life. Lake Chelan Lutheran Church, an American Lutheran congregation in Chelan, provided sanction for celebration of the Sacraments and was Holden's congregation of record. But Holden was too remote geographically to be able to participate in any kind of parish life with the Chelan congregation.

Once a year-round community developed at the Village, it became clear that some other solution was needed. The solution was the formation of Fullness of God Lutheran Church in 1972. Carroll Hinderlie was called as its pastor. It affiliated with the ALC. Affiliation with the Lutheran Church—Missouri Synod and the Lutheran Church in America was also sought, but Lutheran polities would not permit multiple affiliation. Still, in the preamble to its constitution Fullness of God affirmed its understanding that as an ALC congregation it could minister fully to members of the LCMS and the LCA, since the ALC was in pulpit and altar fellowship with both of those national bodies.

Hinderlie was both pastor and chief Village administrator. He had pastoral assistance briefly in 1973 from Arnie Ohaks and Johan Hinderlie, but it was soon apparent that someone was needed who could serve as pastor on a virtually full-time basis. Nancy Winder became that person, serving from 1976 to 1978.

Pastor Winder speaks of the challenge of being pastor at Holden as resembling "ministry to a parade." There is a need to give pastoral care to those who are present on a longer-term basis, something that is more than "just watching buses come and go."

She also understands that a community like Holden Village needs one person who is designated to be sensitive to problems before they grow into crises. "Without that, I can't imagine a small group of people, such as Holden has in the fall, winter, and spring, living in any kind of peace with each other."

Having a congregation at Holden, Nancy believes, "is a way to keep Holden from becoming an idol. There was pressure on Carroll, for example, to be a kind of cult leader. There was pressure to view Holden as something extraordinary. But a parish is an ordinary experience for ordinary sinners, with only a Savior who is extraordinary."

A congregation at Holden in many respects can never be typical. It has its operating expenses entirely absorbed within the regular Village budget, which means it may be the only congregation in American Lutheranism that can give its entire income to ministries beyond itself. Further, it does not have its own church building. The issue of a special building for worship at Holden was raised in the 1960s, and again when Fullness of God was organized.

"I strongly resisted the idea that Holden needed a chapel," says Carroll Hinderlie. "Either this whole place is a chapel or we're missing the point of the Incarnation."

Still, Fullness of God has tried to do some things in the style of a more normal congregation. It elects and sends delegates to the assemblies of the larger church. It takes part in studies of social statement drafts when the national church submits them. It even has an annual congregational picnic outing in the late spring or early fall, usually to the beach at Lucerne.

The other pastors who have been called to serve at Holden are John Schramm (1978-84), James Fish (1978-79), Joel Oines (1980-83), Maynard Johnson (1982-83), Elmer Witt (1984 to present), Susan Kyllo (1985-86), and Barbara Rossing (1986 to present).

## Also a Learning Community

From its beginning Holden has been a learning community, too. There is a conscious effort to integrate learning and celebration at the Village.

The program for children during the summer months is creative and filled with the varied activities made possible by the setting and the resource persons who fill the Village. It was placed into the old schoolhouse in 1966, when the sessions for adults left there and moved to the remodeled Koinonia. Children objected to having their program in what was called "school," so a new name was found. "Narnia" was suggested by Mary Hinderlie, after the "Chronicles of Narnia," the children's books by C. S. Lewis.

A program for teenagers has been available in most summer weeks during the past decade and more. It is called the "Minors Program" and is planned each week by the youth who are present, according to their interests, with the assistance of adult leadership.

The adult learning program has always had a strong focus on the needs of the world and the calling of believers in response to those needs. In recent years, advocacy on global concerns has played a central role. Issues of southern Africa, Central America, the Middle East, the relationship between the Soviet Union and the United States—these and more have had continuing attention.

Worship offerings from the Sunday Eucharist are directed to ministries of the church throughout the world. In 1986, summer gifts of more than $8,000 were shared with the Ko-diakanal International Christian School in India; a youth ministry at Cross Lutheran Church, Milwaukee, serving a predominately Black community; and the Native American Theological Association. The winter community in 1986 gave some $3,000 for the Wenatchee (Washington) Hospitality House, Tacoma Nativity House, St. Stephen's Shelter in Minneapolis, Crosswalk of Spokane, Habitat for Humanity, Jubilee Partners, Hopi Indians Legal Defense Fund, KPBX public radio, Bread for the World, and several Central America projects.

Summer offerings for 1987 were designated for the Lutheran Association of Missionaries and Pilots (Alberta), Lutheran Peace Fellowship (U.S.), and various ministries in Central America. In addition, Fullness of God congregation distributes benevolence gifts ($3,500 during 1986).

The thrust of Holden learning has always been toward the ministry of the people of God in the world. There is continuing commitment to stimulate, encourage, and support that ministry. "We hear often of people who say they are able to keep going in their daily tasks," says Elmer Witt, "because of what Holden has given them."

## Challenges to Community

The gift of community is one of the great blessings Holden can offer. Community there does not provide the option of avoiding people, as one might choose to do in the outside world. That makes community both authentic and a challenge, because one must learn to live with a great diversity of people.

The late Jean Swihart said, "I can find mountains elsewhere. To me Holden is people. I discovered genuine community there for the first time in my life."

Gertrude Norstad claims that for her "Holden has always been the excitement of strangers becoming friends."

David Michel says he has "never found, anywhere, such a high concentration of quality people."

But wherever there is depth of community there are also particular challenges that need to be faced. Elmer Witt lists these areas of continuing tension for the Village community:

• the tension between being an intentional, long-term community and providing a ministry of hospitality for guests who come typically for one week in the summer (and are sometimes resented as "outsiders");

• the problem of classism—drawing distinctions between short-term staff, including summer teachers, and long-term staff and administration;

• keeping a balance for staff between work and growth as a person, theologically and spiritually . . . preserving time for solitude;

• the struggle to let family life have its own integrity, separate from the larger community.

Dan Erlander believes Holden has another special sort of problem. "Holden's chief problem may be that it is over-loved. Some people become so possessive about the place that they are unwilling to accept changes. They want it to stay always as they have known and loved it."

Holden also wrestles with the question of how open to be to people who are in serious need of a healing place. The Village leadership has wanted people to know that, as Werner Janssen puts it, "The Village is always available—a place for people in grief, in transition, in any kind of need. It has been an ideal place for many to get away and be in a supportive community, as a volunteer staff person usually. And the winter provides an opportunity in depth of community that the summer cannot."

Yet, Holden has not been able to welcome everyone. "For the sake of both themselves and our community," says Carroll

Hinderlie, "in rare instances we had to say no to persons who needed specific professional care that the Village could not provide."

On occasion the use of drugs has become an issue. Holden believes that nothing is as potentially destructive of community, and thus its rule has been as near the absolute as anything can be in the Village. Fritz Norstad remembers that in 1977 "I had to ask a group of people who were using drugs to leave, with the understanding that they could return after a month if they abandoned all use of drugs while in the Village. Most of them did return. I felt the drug rule was broadly accepted as legitimate for Holden."

## Rituals of Humor

Among the many community rituals Holden has developed, certainly the dedication ceremonies are high points. There's an unwritten rule that they must include humor.

The tradition may have begun when William Buege dedicated the Village hydro system by apologizing because he was "unable to find the dam rubrics" to fit the occasion.

Or when Howard Hong launched a series of sewage system dedications that has continued into the 1980s. Sewage disposal is serious in the affairs of human communities, and especially so at Holden because of the environment's fragility. Perhaps that's why at Holden it has become an excuse for levity of rather high caliber.

Fritz Norstad rededicated the bowling alley one year by rolling down the now refinished lanes three balls—one each in the name of the Father, the Son, and the Holy Spirit.

And of course the nightly ritual of the post-dinner Beanie sing (named for the late Beanie Lundholm, its developer) would be far less memorable without the unique and clever Holden lyrics. Of the 31 entries in the current songbook, 10

were written by Philip Brunelle or Doris Edmund or the two
of them together. Other lyricists in the booklet include Norman
Habel, Helen Landsverk, and Dick Wilson.

Holden hilarity makes a major contribution to Holden hospitality. The Village has fun while doing its work, which is,
as John Schramm puts it, to be "a worshiping community
whose primary vocation is the ministry of hospitality."

Hilarity and hospitality join together to make Holden Village
the gift that it has become for so many.

Elmer Witt has described Holden's playfulness as akin to
childhood's vacant lots, where young people learn from un-
supervised play. He sees Holden as a "vacant lot for experimenting with ideas, expressing feelings, trying rituals, ex-
panding horizons. It's a place to explore, to disagree, to share,
to argue, to try out old or new outlandish visions of how the
Gospel leads us in unthought-of, unheard-of, and unimagined
ways."

## Going Out with Good Courage

But eventually everyone must leave Holden. Whether it was
a one-week summer visit or three weeks of volunteer staff work
or long-term service of several years, in the end Holden is no
one's continuing city. People always return to what Villagers
call "the real world."

Many, perhaps most, of them leave Holden with their lives
changed significantly and lastingly. Associate Pastor Barbara
Rossing believes those profound changes happen because the
Village offers depth of community illuminated by the Gospel.
"People learn to trust other people here, and thus to trust
themselves. But in the end it all comes down to trusting the
Gospel!"

Many go out of the Village with the words of the Holden
Prayer, a collect used there since 1964. (Written by an Oxford

cleric, the prayer appears in the Lutheran *Service Book and Hymnal*, page 231 and, slightly adapted, in the order for Evening Prayer in the *Lutheran Book of Worship*, page 153.) There is no better way to take leave of this book.

*O Lord God, who has called us, your servants,*
*    to ventures of which we cannot see the ending,*
*    by paths as yet untrodden, through perils unknown,*

*Give us faith to go out with good courage, not knowing*
*    where we go, but only that your hand is leading us,*
*    and your love supporting us,*

*Through Jesus Christ our Lord. Amen.*

# Appendix One: A Holden Chronology

| | |
|---|---|
| c. 8000 B.C. | Last glacier in Railroad Creek Valley melts. |
| c. 4000 B.C. | Volcanic ash and pumice from Glacier Peak eruption blanket valley. |
| 1855 A.D. | James H. Holden born in Springfield, Massachusetts. |
| 1880s | Great Northern and Northern Pacific explore Railroad Creek Valley as possible route through Cascades. |
| 1893 | J. H. Holden begins prospecting in Railroad Creek Valley. |
| 1896 | Holden files claim after ore discovery, Copper Mountain. |
| 19 May 1918 | Holden dies of cancer at Soap Lake, Washington. |
| 1922 | Crooker Perry of Chelan takes control of Holden mine. |
| 1928 | Howe Sound Company leases mine and begins exploratory work. |
| 1930 | Perry sells mine to Howe Sound. |
| 1931 | Howe Sound seeks post office for town of Chelcop. Depression, low copper price stop full development. |
| 1936 | Howe Sound completes main haulage tunnel into Copper Mountain ore body. |
| 1937 | Company builds mine structures and town (now named Holden). |
| 9 April 1938 | First concentrate shipped down Lake Chelan. Holden soon becomes town of 600-plus people. |
| 7 June 1957 | Wesley Prieb in Anchorage reads of planned mine closing, writes his first letter to Howe Sound. |
| 28 June 1957 | Mine's final day of operation. Village abandoned and empty for next three years. |
| 1 April 1958 | Prieb, now student at Seattle LBI, writes second letter to Howe Sound. |
| 1 April 1960 | Prieb writes third letter to Howe Sound, which telegrams offer of property to LBI, confirmed in letter 19 May. |
| early June 1960 | LBI group (E. V. Stime, Randy Stime, E. K. Lunder, David Thorson, Wes Prieb) visit Village. |
| 29 June 1960 | Informal meeting at Gil Berg home, Seattle, leads to formation of feasibility study committee. |
| July 1960 | Visit to Village by Berg, Victor Nelson, Edward Ottum, others with technical expertise. |
| October 1960 | Formal transfer of property from Howe Sound to LBI. |

| | |
|---|---|
| November 1960 | Berg named interim director of Village. |
| December 1960 | Village board organized; Luvern Rieke named chair. Board develops recommendations to national Lutheran youth offices. |
| February 1961 | Articles of incorporation filed for Holden Village, Inc., and Forest Service issues special-use permit. |
| 1 May 1961 | LBI formally transfers title to Holden Village, Inc., retaining one-half of mineral rights. |
| Summer 1961 | First work group, the Forerunners, at Village mid-June to mid-July, led by Bergstrands and Berg. 71 from Augustana Church national convention visit for day (19 June). LBI sponsors four weeks of program (mid-July to mid-August). |
| Summer 1962 | More work campers renovate Village. First full summer of program, with some 1500 visitors, including many Seattle world's fair-goers. |
| Fall 1962 | Winston Camp (miners' village) bulldozed, burned. |
| 1 May 1963 | Carroll Hinderlie begins as executive director; Gil Berg becomes business manager. |
| Summer 1963 | Family program begins to evolve; 2000 participate. |
| 4-6 Sept. 1963 | Reorganized board—five persons named by each of three Lutheran youth departments—has first meeting. Berg thanked for three-plus years of volunteer leadership. Chalet One later named in his honor. |
| November 1963 | Werner Janssen begins work as business manager (serves until 1984). |
| 1964 | Hydroelectric plant produces electricity for first time. Tape ministry is launched when first cassette is recorded. |
| 1965 | Winter avalanche knocks down several outbuildings and power lines (only one to come near Village in last three decades). |
| 1966 | Remodeled lodge becomes Koinonia. First Holden wedding and first winter guests. |
| January 1969 | Chalet Two burns. |
| 1970-71 | Holden becomes group home for boys. |
| 1971 | Formal association with national Lutheran youth offices ends. Tenth anniversary of retreat center observed. |
| 1972 | Fullness of God congregation organized. |
| 1972-73 | Lifestyle Enrichment, first full winter program, offered. |

| | |
|---|---|
| Spring 1977 | Fritz Norstad becomes interim director after departure of Carroll Hinderlie. |
| 13 August 1977 | Reunion attended by 230 former mining residents marks 20th anniversary of mine closing. |
| April 1978 | John Schramm becomes second permanent director. |
| 1982 | Tekoa plan for Holden communities outside Village is developed. |
| April 1984 | Elmer Witt becomes third permanent director. |
| 1985 | Tekoa Landing community is discontinued. |
| 1986 | Construction of new sewer system begins. |
| July 1987 | Intercultural "Rainbow on the Mountaintop" weeks are offered. |

# Appendix Two: Holden Leadership

## Board Chairpersons

Gilbert Berg (interim committee), 1960
Luvern Rieke, 1960-78
Ellen Gamrath, 1978-86
Duane Lansverk, 1986-

## Executive Directors

Gilbert Berg (interim), 1961-63
Carroll L. Hinderlie, 1963-77
Fredric M. Norstad (interim), 1977-78
John Schramm, 1978-84
Elmer Witt, 1984-

# Appendix Three: Attendance Data

| Year | Avg. Daily Population June-August | People Days Jan.-April & Oct.-December | Total Population for Year | People Days for Year |
|------|------|------|------|------|
| 1961 | | | 500 | |
| 1962 | | | 1600 | |
| 1963 | | | 2460 | 6150 |
| 1964 | 172 | | 2552 | 8242 |
| 1965 | 231 | | 2721 | 16475 |
| 1966 | 214 | | 2817 | 20044 |
| 1967 | 201 | | 2198 | 18953 |
| 1968 | 201 | | 2930 | 23800 |
| 1969 | 280 | | 4252 | 34659 |
| 1970 | 301 | | 3989 | 36872 |
| 1971 | 283 | | 4587 | 44085 |
| 1972 | 319 | 13384 | 4621 | 50653 |
| 1973 | 336 | 12804 | 5283 | 52456 |
| 1974 | 343 | 12731 | 5575 | 53774 |
| 1975 | 321 | 16746 | 5416 | 58213 |
| 1976 | 333 | 17474 | 4906 | 59002 |
| 1977 | 315 | 17236 | 5382 | 58611 |
| 1978 | 340 | 15668 | 5242 | 55988 |
| 1979 | 342 | 16220 | 5374 | 57737 |
| 1980 | 338 | 12485 | 5160 | 54062 |
| 1981 | 354 | 11907 | 5435 | 54840 |
| 1982 | 358 | 18273 | 5983 | 63400 |
| 1983 | 345 | 16809 | 6099 | 60414 |
| 1984 | 333 | 15823 | 5778 | 57252 |
| 1985 | 330 | 15440 | 5117 | 54475 |
| 1986 | 352 | 15868 | 5511 | 57621 |

# Appendix Four: Correspondence Between Wes Prieb and Howe Sound

Wesley H. Prieb
Engineer Supply Depot
APO—Anchorage, Alaska

June 7, 1957

Howe Sound Mining Company
Holden, Washington
Attention: Manager

Dear Sir:

It has come to my attention that Holden Village is presently being abandoned by the Howe Sound Company and that the mine is closing.

I would appreciate it if you would send information regarding the asking price of this property. This property could be useful for a church summer camp, or a camp that could be used as a retreat center. It would be appreciated if you would send any information that might be available.

Thank you for your kind help.

Very sincerely,
Wesley H. Prieb

Howe Sound Company
500 Fifth Ave.
New York, N.Y.

June 14, 1957

Dear Mr. Prieb,

In answer to your letter of June 7, 1957, we are replying to advise you that Holden Village is priced for sale at $100,000.

If there is any other information that you might desire, please do not hesitate to write or inquire. Thank you for your interest in Holden Village.

Very sincerely,

Daniel J. Roper
Superintendent, Holden Mine

Wesley H. Prieb
Lutheran Bible Institute
13016 Greenwood Avenue
Seattle 33, Washington

April 1, 1958

Howe Sound Company
Chelan, Washington

Dear Mr. Roper:

I am writing again to inquire about the status of the Holden Village property, and whether this property has been sold.

It would seem that this property would be ideal for use as a summer camp, a retreat center for the general use of the church and the Lutheran Bible Institute.

Any information regarding the present asking price and the status of Holden Village would be very much appreciated.

Very sincerely,

Wesley H. Prieb

Howe Sound Company
Chelan Division
Chelan, Washington

April 5, 1958

Dear Mr. Prieb:

This is in answer to your letter of April 1, 1958. We are writing to advise you that Holden Village is available for the price of $100,000. All equipment is in place and the hospital equipment is available and is stored in Chelan.

Thank you for your interest in Holden Village.

Very sincerely yours,

Daniel J. Roper


Wesley H. Prieb
Lutheran Bible Institute
13016 Greenwood Avenue
Seattle 33, Washington

April 1, 1960

Howe Sound Company
Chelan, Washington

Dear Mr. Roper:

I am writing to inquire about the status of Holden Village at Chelan, Washington. I believe that this property might be a desirable place for the use of the church or the Lutheran Bible Institute as a summer camp. The church needs a camp which could be used for our young people.

Information pertaining to the price presently being asked, the status or any other information will be deeply appreciated.

Thank you for your kind help and information.

Very sincerely yours,

Wesley H. Prieb


Telegram to:

Wesley H. Prieb
Lutheran Bible Institute, Seattle

YOUR LETTER RECEIVED. PLEASE CALL OUR OFFICE SALT LAKE CITY COLLECT. MR. KIRKLAND, MAGNUM, UTAH.

A. G. Kirkland
Magnum, Utah

# Bibliography

Adams, Nigel B. *The Holden Mine: Discovery to Production, 1896-1938* (Wenatchee, Washington: Washington State Historical Society and World Publishing, 1981).

Edmund, Rudolph W. *The Mine—Holden Village* (Chelan: Holden Village pamphlet, undated).

Hong, Edna. "Two Who Shaped Holden Village" in *Tapestry,* edited by Wilfred C. Bockelman (Minneapolis: Augsburg, 1985, pp. 43-46).

_____, Minutes of Holden Village Board of Directors, 1960-86.

Prieb, Wesley H. *The Holden Story as Told by Wes Prieb* (Chelan: Holden Village Press, 1974).

_____, *Reports and Actions of The American Lutheran Church,* 1962, 1964, 1966, 1968, 1970 (Minneapolis: Office of the Secretary, The American Lutheran Church).